Essentials of Thinking Ethically in Qualitative Research

Qualitative Essentials

Series Editor:
Janice Morse, *University of Utah*

Series Editorial Board: *H. Russell Bernard, Kathy Charmaz, D. Jean Clandinin, Juliet Corbin, Carmen de la Cuesta, John Engel, Sue E. Estroff, Jane Gilgun, Jeffrey C. Johnson, Carl Mitcham, Katja Mruck, Judith Preissle, Jean J. Schensul, Sally Thorne, John Van Maanen, Max van Manen*

Qualitative Essentials is a book series providing a comprehensive but succinct overview of topics in qualitative inquiry. These books will fill an important niche in qualitative methods for students—and others new to the qualitative research—who require rapid but complete perspective on specific methods, strategies, and important topics. Written by leaders in qualitative inquiry, alone or in combination, these books are an excellent resource for instructors and students from all disciplines. Proposals for the series should be sent to the series editor at explore@lcoastpress.com.

Titles in this series:

1. *Naturalistic Observation*, Michael V. Angrosino
2. *Essentials of Qualitative Inquiry*, Maria J. Mayan
3. *Essentials of Field Relationships*, Amy Kaler and Melanie A. Beres
4. *Essentials of Accessible Grounded Theory*, Phyllis Norerager Stern and Caroline Jane Porr
5. *Essentials of Qualitative Interviewing*, Karin Olson
6. *Essentials of Transdisciplinary Research*, Patricia Leavy
7. *Essentials of Focus Groups*, Martha Ann Carey and Jo-Ellen Asbury
8. *Essentials of a Qualitative Doctorate*, Immy Holloway and Lorraine Brown
9. *Focus Group Research*, Martha Ann Carey and Jo-Ellen Asbury
10. *Essentials of Thinking Ethically in Qualitative Research*, Will C. van den Hoonaard and Deborah K. van den Hoonaard

Essentials of Thinking Ethically in Qualitative Research

Will C. van den Hoonard and
Deborah K. van den Hoonaard

Routledge
Taylor & Francis Group

LONDON AND NEW YORK

First published 2013 by Left Coast Press, Inc.

Published 2016 by Routledge
2 Park Square, Milton Park, Abingdon, Oxon OX14 4RN
711 Third Avenue, New York, NY 10017, USA

Routledge is an imprint of the Taylor & Francis Group, an informa business

Library of Congress Cataloging-in-Publication Data:

Van den Hoonaard, Will. C. (Willy Carl), 1942–
 Essentials of thinking ethically in qualitative research / Will C. van den Hoonaard and Deborah K. van den Hoonaard.
     pages cm. — (Qualitative essentials ; 10)
 Includes bibliographical references.
 ISBN 978-1-61132-204-0 (hardback : alk. paper) — ISBN 978-1-61132-205-7 (pbk. : alk. paper) — ISBN 978-1-61132-714-4 (consumer ebook)
 1. Qualitative research. 2. Social sciences—Research. I. Van den Hoonaard, Deborah K. (Deborah Kestin), 1951– II. Title.
 H62.V293 2013
 174'.900142--dc23

                    2012048861

ISBN 978-1-61132-204-0 hardcover
ISBN 978-1-61132-205-7 paperback

Contents

Dedicated to Rosemary Clews (1944–2012)

Without her influence on our lives,
this book would never have been written.

Preface

Essentials of Thinking Ethically in Qualitative Research will, we hope, provide a sound basis from which students will feel empowered to make ethical judgments when doing qualitative research. Just as one cannot separate relevant ethical principles from larger societal considerations, one cannot consider their appropriateness without understanding the nature of qualitative research. To that end, the book brings into relief both the larger social structures that impinge on research and the intent of qualitative research. Standing between both is you, the researcher, who must adopt an inner ethical poise that brings the research to a successful conclusion.

Readers will discover that this ethical poise requires ongoing reflection. Just as qualitative research is always an emergent process, so are the ethical dimensions of the research constantly emerging and shifting. Essentials of Thinking Ethically identifies relevant ethical principles that can guide researchers through qualitative research and help them complete their research with the necessary wisdom and insight that have the potential to contribute to and shape the research conversation in sound, meaningful, and thoughtful ways. Readers will soon notice that we have relied on the experiences of qualitative researchers in many fields to grasp what it means to conduct ethical research.

van den Hoonaard, Will C., and Deborah K. van den Hoonaard, "Preface," in *Essentials of Thinking Ethically in Qualitative Research*, pp. 7–9. © 2013 Left Coast Press, Inc. All rights reserved.

This textbook represents a departure from other approaches to ethics in research. Its point of departure is what happens "on the ground," that is, the lived experience of researchers as they undertake the challenging task of making ethical judgments fit with their research, and vice versa.

Our textbook is not a pious rendering of what ethics codes say about research. Although we have not written it as a handbook on how to submit proposals to university ethics committees, we do touch upon issues surrounding formal ethics frameworks and suggest ways that novice (and veteran) qualitative researchers can maintain ethical sensitivity as they conform to regulatory regimes.

The first set of chapters deals with the general characteristics of qualitative research in relation to research ethics. Chapter 1 provides an overall introduction to qualitative research and highlights its most distinguishing features. Chapter 2 explores ethical prisms in relation to research participants, gathering and handling data, and the dissemination of research findings. Chapter 3 touches on confidentiality, anonymity, and consent.

The second set of chapters relates ethics to the most commonly used strategies of qualitative research. Each chapter provides an overview of a particular strategy, brings in the ethical principles enumerated above, and explores and discusses their relevance to the strategy at hand. Chapter 4 delves into doing fieldwork, and Chapter 5 considers the ethical components of doing interviews, autoethnographies, and focus groups. Chapter 6 explores Internet research as the newest venue for doing qualitative research, while Chapter 7 deals with photo elicitation. Chapter 8 delves into one of the most misunderstood aspects of research, covert research.

The third set of chapters looks at the ethical contexts of conducting research in particular social settings. By virtue of curiosity, qualitative researchers explore many social settings, each beckoning them to take into account a different set of ethics. This part touches on some of the most frequently researched contexts, namely those of vulnerability, marginality, and disability (Chapter 9), often involving research with children or inmates; organizational and institutional contexts (Chapter 10); and qualitative health research (Chapter 11). Chapter 12, which explores writing, publication, and (re)presentation, implicates the research participant, the researcher, and the readers of her work.

The fourth and final set of chapters brings in a discussion about compliance with formal ethics frameworks. Whatever the designation of ethics committees (institutional review boards in the United States, research ethics boards in Canada, local ethics committees in the United Kingdom, and human research ethics committees in Australia), they may evoke trepidation, fear, and disappointment. However, they also offer opportunities for graduate students to probe the relevance of their theories, topics, and strategies to gain a more profound understanding of ethics and of the meaning and purpose of qualitative research. Chapter 13 discusses the process of formal research-ethics review, and Chapter 14 briefly considers "ethics lag," whereby the routines and exigencies of contemporary and emerging research practices outstrip ethics policies.

Acknowledgments

We wish to acknowledge our gratitude to Janice M. Morse, series editor, who invited us to author this textbook for PhD students. Her commitment to ethics in research is well known, yielding gems of useful insights on the nature of research ethics. We also thank Mitch Allen, the publisher of Left Coast Press, for providing us with an avenue of publishing our ideas about what it means to conduct ethical research.

At the Atlantic Centre for Qualitative Research and Analysis (St. Thomas University, Fredericton, New Brunswick, Canada), we benefited from the research assistance of Amanda Merrithew. Lehanne Knowlton, staff member extraordinaire at the Centre, provided us with her insights, office and editorial help, and a sense of humor to bring this book project to fruition.

Riva Soucie and Linda Caissie provided us with useful advice about sections of the book that involved their own research–and we thank them heartfully. We also thank Karitas Þrainsdottir of Kopavógur, Iceland, for verifying our information on Iceland (in Chapter 3).

We both owe a note of thanks to St. Thomas University and the University of New Brunswick (both in Fredericton) for providing a collegial atmosphere in which to conduct our research and writing. We should also thank the many researchers, too many to name, who have shared their stories and ethical dilemmas with us, either directly or through their publications.

Chapter One

Introduction

Qualitative research was born in the shadow of anthropology. As early as the nineteenth century, Western anthropologists conceived of the idea of studying cultures holistically, albeit with the early belief that such studies should have a positivist basis. With the enthusiastic discovery of non-Western cultures, ethical reflection and practices took a backseat; it might be more accurate to say that early anthropologists did not entertain careful ethical thought that should have pervaded all of their work in exotic locations (or from an armchair). As Murray Wax (1980: 272) points out, the accounts of such well-known anthropologists as Margaret Mead and Bronislaw Malinowski (in Samoa and Trobriand Islands, respectively) provide us with the image of the "solitary anthropologist" living "intimately within a community of 'Stone Age' people." "The anthropologist," Wax claims, "learns and participates in an exotic way of life and then returns to report to colleagues and the literate public."

Over time, anthropology, with the help of sociology, gave way to the study of communities and groups and realized the need to prioritize the perspectives of these studied social entities. A high degree of "exoticism" pervaded many of these early studies, which reinforced the idea of "othering" cultures. Today, qualitative researchers challenge the whole concept of "othering" because it runs counter to doing interpretive and inductive research.

By the early 1950s, this approach had already dictated the sociological impetus to study contemporary urban Western cultures, such as those of funeral directors (Habenstein, 1954), gangs (Whyte, 1955), prisons, mental asylums, factories, small towns, schools, and so on (Wax, 1980: 272).

In the course of time, other disciplines adopted this approach, giving rise to a large array of qualitative techniques, each one uniquely expressing the tenor of each discipline: narrative research, discourse analysis, participant observation, case studies, ethnography, photo elicitation, and so on (Denzin and Lincoln, 1994: 3). Now it is common to find researchers in psychology, nursing, education, and social work who engage in qualitative research. What all of these approaches share is the search for meanings that research participants exemplify through their words and deeds. It is an inductive approach that, ideally speaking, takes its cues from the world of the people who are being studied. In many respects, this approach differs widely from those early anthropological approaches driven by the belief that there is an objective reality that scientists can uncover, describe, and analyze. A very different scholarly world indeed.

No less divergent have been the contemporary ethical stances towards the study of communities, groups, and cultures, whether in the field or as expressed through text. These stances represent a whole range of subtle hues, depending on the discipline, the researcher (including the researcher's own culture), the researched setting, the nature of groups that are being studied, and the strategies of research. The "growing recognition that we cannot represent others in any other terms but our own" (Van Maanen, 1988: 12) underscores a heightened need to engage in an ethical conversation within ourselves lest we mistake our understanding of others as infallible or "objective."

It will be nigh impossible, except for a few broad principles, to outline specifically the definite ethical parameters that undergird all qualitative research. When one is more familiar with the ethical canons of either quantitative or biomedical research, it is easy to be apprehensive when being confronted with the ethical peculiarities of qualitative research. Qualitative researchers do not claim to be exempt from the importance of ethics in research. Although some general ethics principles do apply, a qualitative researcher's approach often involves different issues and solutions calling upon other kinds of ethical principles that are particularly relevant in their case. For example, a qualitative researcher usually embraces whole groups or communities as part of her[1] study, rather than individuals on a one-to-one basis. As another example, it is hard to pin down the precise nature or goals of one's research—an aspect that has an impact on how she explains the research to others.

At the heart of thinking ethically is the need to grasp the nature of qualitative research. Following Herbert G. Blumer (1969), qualitative researchers understand society as an "obdurate reality" because as Gary A. Fine (1993) exclaims, society is secured in secrets, often beyond the pale of the casual observer. We thus need a method that probes issues more deeply. These uncertainties make our grasp of society fluid, but they also lead every conscientious researcher to move beneath the initial surface (appearance) of society.

As such, the qualitative researcher places great value on modifying her research plan along the way as she deepens her understanding of the setting. Often, there are surprising, unexpected, and unpredictable sources of data of a serendipitous nature. New horizons open to the researcher. It is quite impossible to predict or anticipate the ethical dimensions that may arise in the course of such changes. Hence, one needs to cultivate one's inner ethical poise, which can carry her through the challenges of doing qualitative research in the ever-changing social context or situation. One stands to benefit from knowing the experiences of other researchers who have taken a similar path of research. Indeed, one purpose of *The Essentials of Thinking Ethically* is to bring readers' attention to a number of their studies.

Ethics in research does not take place in a vacuum. Ethics is about relationships. Before considering how particular research strategies involve ethics, we need to explore ethics as expressed through the four main prisms of qualitative research: namely, the researcher, relations with research participants, data gathering, and the dissemination of research findings. Each prism calls for specific ethical obligations and rights. We also need to provide a broad discussion of confidentiality. This discussion involves sizing up its shape, much like one takes into account the morphology of the ground. This last discussion concludes the first part of this book.

Summary

Born in the bosom of anthropology as "fieldwork," qualitative research rose and evolved through a variety of disciplines, including sociology, social work, education, and health research. All have their own distinctive features, but they all share the idea of inductive research. In contrast, however, to the earlier anthropological research, today's research does not claim to be objective and challenges the whole idea of "othering." Once researchers reject "othering," a new ethical conversation needs to be started. Moreover, the need to modify one's research plans as the research moves forward forces researchers to become agents of their own ethical practice. A textbook such as ours relies on the experiences of researchers as they have come face-to-face with ethical issues; for better or worse, the textbook cannot rely completely on national ethics guidelines or codes because they mainly use a biomedical frame of reference. The unique feature of the book primarily consists of its reliance on the ethics experience of qualitative researchers, buttressed by research-ethics codes.

Chapter Two

Ethical Prisms

This chapter explains the general and particular characteristics of qualitative research that require special approaches to ethical reflection. There are, however, many distractions that can cloud this reflection: the researcher's own cultural background, the appearance of doing "proper" research, lack of time to gather and analyze data, unexpected encounters in the social setting, and disciplinary and institutional pressures, to name a few. While this book articulates the germane ethical principles of respecting human dignity, respecting persons, and being concerned for welfare and justice, there are also a number of distinctive ways that the ethical journey differs in qualitative research. This journey touches the researcher, relations with research participants, data gathering, and dissemination of research findings.

An examination of national ethics codes pertaining to research reveals no shortage of clearly established ethical principles. In England, for example, Rachel Aldred (2008: 889) reminds us that six core principles should govern social research, namely "(1) integrity and quality; (2) full disclosure about the research to research staff and subjects; (3) confidentiality and anonymity; (4) voluntary participation by participants; (5) avoidance of harm of participants and; (6) avoiding or disclosing conflicts of interest." Elizabeth Murray and Robert Dingwall

(2002: 339) reaffirm some of these ethical principles in research when they emphasize the importance of *non-maleficence* (researchers should avoid harming participants), *beneficence* (research on human subjects should produce some positive and identifiable benefit rather than simply be carried out for its own sake), *autonomy* or *self-determination* (the values and decisions of research participants should be respected), and *justice* (people who are equal in relevant respects should be treated equally). A researcher can find similar principles in the *Belmont Report* (National Commission, 1979), which is used as the basis for ethical guidelines in the United States.

Our task, however, is to apply and correlate these principles to the demands and needs of qualitative research/-ers. The astute reader will have already noted that the ideologies of individualism, individual autonomy, and self-determination have come alive in these general principles. *Essentials of Thinking Ethically* hopes to offer a negotiated settlement between these generic, individualistically based principles and the nature of qualitative research that underscores, without any hesitation, the *social* basis of research.

Kathleen Blee and Ashley Currier (2011: 404) offer sage advice when it comes to seeing ethics in terms of "disallowed actions." The researcher sets limits on what he can take down as data. Identifying, for example, a coal miner's sexual orientation might bring real danger to that person. While these "negative, preemptive orientations" to ethics forestall a situation that could be "brimming with harm" and are good in "sidestepping ethical calamities," they also allow the researcher to think more deeply about the relationship between positive and negative findings, between seeking out people who wish to take front stage versus those who desire to remain in the shadows. These ethical conundrums are also scholarly as one comes to terms with the purpose and nature of one's own research.

The Researcher

The researcher endeavors to be honest in his relationships with colleagues; admits to errors, missteps, and mistakes; and confesses the pressures of scholarship he is experiencing. He is trustworthy; takes time to do research, analysis, and writing; and values integrity when doing the analysis. This ethical inner poise can be difficult to maintain as competitive outlooks, the pressures of time, and prepublication secrecy might incline one to surrender that ethical poise. What is more problematic, from a moral perspective, are the mixed motivations that are intrinsic to research. A number of experienced researchers have pondered this particular problem. Can "honesty" be the best policy when our motives for doing the research are fraught with reasons that we do not discuss with participants (Wax, 1980: 277)? Is our self-presentation to participants really us (Fine, 1993)? And is the researcher's moral accounting based on self-serving, pragmatic considerations? Does not the researcher ask himself whether this or that behavior helps his research (Bosk, 2001: 203)? Are our friendships natural or are they directed towards a particular goal in research?

Relations with Research Participants

In terms of relations with research participants, the researcher must consider such highly fluctuating ethical dimensions as voluntary participation, anonymity, and confidentiality. These can be ambiguous dimensions. Thinking about power and recognizing actual or potential inequality are yet other ingredients of thinking ethically. Because qualitative research may take a long time, it is not unusual that relations with research participants change over time, creating ethical dimensions hitherto unthought-of. After a researcher has induced professional interactions with research participants, such interactions can become personal, sometimes highly personal, as the researcher becomes more and more integrated into the social setting. Even after the research is over, a researcher will fluctuate in his beliefs regarding whether or not he should maintain these natural relationships of friendship. Moreover, relations with research participants of higher social standing can induce unexpected ethical dilemmas that are different than with members of marginal groups. In the case of researching elites, there are veils of secrecy that the researcher must traverse, and he must decide what secrets should be opened up for publication. The stakes of confidentiality are high (Odendahl and Shaw, 2001), and in the case of researching marginal groups, there is a tendency to side with them, and sometimes to become their advocate, which changes the ethical nature of the relationship.

Power in human relationships seems inevitable. The crux of a feminist approach to ethical research resides in the relationship of power between the researcher and research participant. Tina Miller and Linda Bell (2002: 54) highlight the imbalance of power in the case of violent relationships in the lives of research participants (which become apparent when a researcher interviews partners of violent men). But when it comes down to the relationships between the researcher and the participant, the feminist approach seeks reciprocity between the two, in addition to empowering the participant (Miller and Bell, 2002: 65).

Only when there are attempts to (re)negotiate the power imbalance between the researcher and the research participant will the nature and force of consent be known and recognized. Research participants may find themselves consenting to more than they had originally agreed (Miller and Bell, 2002: 54). For example, the researcher might anticipate their reading their own transcripts—an onerous job, involving many hours of extra work.

To undertake research antagonistic to our own ethical poise can raise grave concerns. Do we maintain that poise or do we suspend our moral judgments (Wax, 1980: 277)? Both are possible. There is no social phenomenon that some researcher does not carry antipathies towards. When one considers the fact that everyone works within a social structure, it follows that one must imagine a moral hierarchy: a street felon works within the structure of a gang, and that gang operates within a larger social matrix. It is indeed a poor form of research to imagine that a research participant functions only in terms of himself and that he works outside a social web of relations. The notion that we are all intermeshed in a social structure should allow us to undertake research antagonistic to our moral sensibilities because the locus is not the individual but the social structure. Whether one researches wealthy or poor people, "deviants" or "normals," the qualitative researcher understands that an individual's location and attributes can only make sense when larger social forces, that is, social structure, are taken into account.

The idea of harm is very prevalent when it comes to doing any kind of research. As Lisa McIntyre avers in *The Practical Skeptic* (2002: 50), there is potential for harm in any sort of research that involves human subjects, but aside from the most evident example of harm (e.g., physical), it may not be easy to determine such harm, whether by what we do, what we do not do, or what we neglect to do. An interview, for example, fraught with deeply emotional elements, can mirror a sense of a highly connected relationship that offers the research participant the opportunity to tell her side of a story that family or friends have ignored or misunderstood. Lisa Tillmann-Healy (2003: 745) says that such a connection with research participants can elicit "fears and concerns," but one can "listen closely and respond compassionately." In the end, the researcher can "use such exchanges to refine the study and direct its implications." Even in the instance of Laud Humphreys' *The Tearoom Trade* (1970), a study much criticized for the surreptitious and deceptive methods by which he gained his data about impersonal sexual activity, one could argue that, in the end, his research led to a greater awareness of the existence of homosexuality and contributed to more enlightened policies that decriminalized homosexuality (McIntyre, 2002: 51). Just as the researcher should not rush to the conclusion that his research contains no harm, neither should he dismiss the possibility that the research might be harmful to research participants. Any research involves triggers that underscore the potential harm, but those trigger points are sometimes quite invisible until it is too late.

Perhaps no other relation with research participants evokes deeper ethical reflection than friendship. It is natural when researchers do field research to construct, maintain, and sometimes even end friendships. Lisa Tillmann-Healy (2003: 734) points to the "practices of friendship" through which one gathers data. She identifies friendship as an integral part of doing field research. Gary Fine (1993), however, offers a more sobering ethical reflection about friendships in the field: every type of work involves illusions, and research in the field is no exception. Researchers believe in idealized benchmarks when doing ethical fieldwork, such as being virtuous and technically competent.

Gathering and Handling Data

No less important are the ethical issues surrounding the gathering and handling of data. What comes to the fore is the ever-changing requirement to think ethically as the means of gathering and analyzing data change over time. The researcher is mindful of the relevance of the hierarchy of credibility when gathering data. In a brilliant essay, Howard S. Becker (Debro, 1986: 38–39; Becker, 1967)[2] reminds us that a researcher might be inclined to regard information or data from individuals with a higher status as more relevant. One assumes that these individuals are people "in the know." Would not a prison warden have more knowledge than a prison inmate about the situation in prisons? Would a social worker know more about the experience of homelessness than a person who is homeless? Researchers must guard against this tendency to rely on "expert" opinion. Everybody who accepts the legitimacy of a hierarchy will also accept the idea that those higher in the hierarchy will have a credibility that others lack. A researcher has thus a special obligation to be mindful of that hierarchy when seeking and analyzing data.

Collecting qualitative data is not a smooth process. Far from it. One of our colleagues, Rose McCloskey (2011), conducted a participant-observation study about the transfer of older residents of a nursing home to a hospital emergency room and vice versa. What struck her were the many anomalies of those trips to and from the hospital. One day, she returned to her office in the nursing home and found someone had anonymously left her an envelope containing vital information. Should she use or ignore the data in that envelope? What settled her moral quandary was her realization that whoever left the envelope must have gone through a lot of effort for someone who was afraid of potential repercussions. To ignore it would be an insult to that invisible research participant who thought it was important to get the information to the researcher without identifying him- or herself (cf. Crow et al., 2006: 93).

Dissemination of Research Findings

We often do not think about the dissemination of findings as part of the research process that involves ethics. Dissemination, so we think, comes at the end of a long process. However, a number of ethical issues quickly come to fruition especially at the point when results of research are published. Researchers resort to using pseudonyms instead of real names of research participants, but true anonymity is hard to come by. Dissemination of research brings into focus critical research (as a potential "problem" for research participants), the potentially invasive role of funding bodies, the extent to which research participants share the process of dissemination, and the dignity of the reader—an issue that is rarely, if ever, dealt with in formal ethics guidelines.

The qualitative researcher must contend with the fact that much of the data he has gathered do not come from anonymous sources. The researcher resorts to coining pseudonyms, the most common practice in disguising one's research sources. When Deborah van den Hoonaard wrote *The Widowed Self* (2001), she made a special effort to come up with pseudonyms that correlated with the relevant names that were typical of the time when these women were born. Another researcher, Dawne Clarke, assigned pseudonyms to her research participants based on the characters of her favorite television show, *Coronation Street*. Will van den Hoonaard selected pseudonyms based on the temperaments or personality similar to his friends and acquaintances. Disguising research participants is sometimes not as easy as it might seem at first. Sometimes, a research participant insists that the researcher use his real name in a publication, thereby potentially exposing the whole group under study.

Changing biographical details constitutes another way of ensuring the research participants' anonymity. Research in small groups or settings already poses a serious difficulty in maintaining anonymity (W. van den Hoonaard, 2003), and thus the researcher might devise the best manner of keeping certain recognizable biographical details at arm's length. One's best efforts are required to create anonymity. Joyce Kennedy (2005) found it particularly challenging to write up her research on hearing-impaired students in a regional school devoted to serving this kind of student. It became an ethical puzzle for her to describe a boy with hearing disabilities playing on a soccer team without identifying him in her research. Not only would everyone in the region immediately recognize the school, but the children attending that school, and their parents, would also recognize him.

Research that challenges the status quo—and some claim that if one's research does not have such a character, it has not fulfilled its task—will inevitably raise eyebrows if not in the studied community then among some individual research participants. Research entails open inquiry falling under academic freedom. One might explore areas that shed light on circumstances that research participants do not wish to be raised. How does one handle a critical perspective when reporting on one's research? For research to have credibility, it will be necessary to frankly set out those circumstances. Is it possible without hurting the sensibilities of research participants who have opened up their world to you, the researcher?

Solving this problem goes to the heart of all good research, but it requires the researcher to make an initial assessment about the extent to which he can allow himself to maintain academic freedom in his research. If the research setting prevents him from achieving that goal, and he believes he cannot live with the consequences or believes the honesty of his research will be compromised, he must forego that particular direction of research and find a more suitable setting where his integrity will not be compromised. If, however, he finds the research setting too important to abandon, a number of alternatives will surface.

First, much can be said in the publication of research when the research does not portray individuals as the source of difficulties and keeps in mind the relevance of the social structure that permits the difficulties to be maintained. Second, the researcher should realize that his understanding of a setting is influenced by his own convictions and personal discovery, and that his perspective is one of several. This realization induces the researcher to offer a balanced, more nuanced perspective that serves to enhance understanding rather than provoke more difficulties.[3]

One might ask the extent to which research participants involve themselves in the work of reporting one's research. Given the diversity of approaches in qualitative research, the answer is not a straightforward one. On one hand, participatory-action research insists that no analysis can be complete without the research participants' own understanding or analysis of the findings. On the other hand, there are researchers who claim that the publishing of findings is the researchers' responsibility, not the research participants'. In that light, researchers base their findings and analysis on having spoken to numerous people in various research settings, presumably seeing more social patterns at play than any one individual. There are, moreover, situations involving research among aboriginal peoples that require the researcher to make special arrangements involving decisions on the topics to be studied, ownership of data, and responsibility of analysis—all contingent on the positive outcome of a consultation with the appropriate community.

Thus, as we can see, researchers have come up with a number of literary and writing devices that can potentially diminish the problem of academic compromise. Some researchers go to great lengths to soften the critical reports of research findings by, for example, giving research participants a voice in the analysis itself. In some cases, the style and format of writing can handle these kinds of difficulties. A researcher buries controversial issues that are not germane to the research in an endnote or footnote. In other instances, the researcher couches the critical issue as distant as possible from the person who provided that information.

The increasing university reliance on privately obtained sources of funds for research creates a need to shape its own ethical sphere that can safeguard the integrity that comes with publishing one's research. The funding body prevents the publication of one's research or the publication of one's work will be buried in a governmental archive. The prestige attached to receiving significant funding can potentially override any concerns with integrity and honesty. On a more subtle level, the funding organization or agency defines the problem to be investigated. A researcher may be called upon to do a study of cheating among students, but defines the problem in such a manner that it will be impossible to implicate the school or teachers, for example. Such an approach compromises the published results of that research. A narrow definition of a topic to be funded for research might not give the researcher any conceptual or methodological leeway.

But publishing one's research involves yet another audience, namely the reader, who is not involved in the research itself. The finest examples of writing express a dignity for the reader. The researcher writes in a tone that allows the reader the freedom to make up his own mind.

Summary

National codes around the world share many similar principles of conducting ethical research, such things as maintaining human dignity, respecting persons, and promoting welfare and justice. However, the distinctive aspects of qualitative research call for a distinctive ethical reflection. In the main, qualitative researchers need to move away from the individually based concepts in ethics codes and embrace concepts that have a social basis. This chapter explored how these principles operate from the perspective of the researcher, relations with research participants, gathering and handling data, and disseminating research findings. The researcher enters the research setting with mixed motivation, which complicates his ethical reflection. In terms of research participants, the qualitative researcher readily understands that such notions as voluntary participation, anonymity, confidentiality, and harm are ambiguous. Relations of power and inequality provide a further challenge to ethical reflection. Moreover, the researcher always gains data that can steer the issue of ethics in any given direction. Often, data stem from a hierarchy of credibility that devalues the experiences and opinions of those who are not at the top of that hierarchy. Finally, the chapter pointed to the problem of studying small settings (where it is a challenge to maintain anonymity). Even changing biographical details proves to be difficult.

Chapter Three

Confidentiality, Anonymity, and Consent

A Mutable Triangle

onfidentiality, anonymity, and consent compose the triangle of ethics in research. While few will disagree with these tenets, the circumstances and social context of the research and the social location of research participants can bend the triangle into another shape.

Many consider the right to privacy the bedrock or cornerstone of a free, just, and peaceful society (Seifert and Shute, 2005). The Universal Declaration of Human Rights of the United Nations expresses this right as follows: "no one shall be subjected to arbitrary interference with his [or her] privacy, family, home or correspondence . . . [and] everyone has the right to the protection of the law against such interference" (United Nations, 1948: Article 12). The bulwark against the invasion of privacy is confidentiality and anonymity.

This chapter elaborates on how qualitative researchers have approached confidentiality and anonymity. It explores the challenge of the researcher's maintaining confidentiality as she encounters everyday breaches of confidentiality in public and semipublic spaces and in daily routines. How does she scrupulously follow the mandate of confidentiality while evidence in everyday life suggests the contrary? Should the researcher hold herself to a higher standard, or would it be more realistic to follow popular dictates?

The question of anonymity is more complex. For a large number of empirical reasons, a qualitative researcher will feel particularly challenged to maintain anonymity even though it is urgent to do so. Research in villages, rural areas, total institutions, or illegal settings is unlikely to be able to maintain anonymity. Moreover, research on sensitive topics, in particular, requires the cloak of anonymity.

The process of consent can be vagarious, reflecting the exigencies of particular methodologies, circumstances, and settings. It is not an uncommon experience for a researcher to discover that research participants derive an understanding from the consent process different from what the researcher had intended. Formal, legal approaches to obtaining consent can yield suspicion on the part of the participant and, as a consequence, throw the whole interaction between the researcher and the participant into an unwarranted and unintended direction, and thereby entirely miss the point of research.

The Landscape of Confidentiality

Confidentiality appears to override virtually every other consideration in ethical research. According to Russel Ogden (2008: 111), confidentiality means "that information shared with researchers will not be disclosed in a way that can publicly identify a participant or source." Without the protection of confidentiality, following Ogden, people can be embarrassed, harmed, or stigmatized, especially when research entails such sensitive topics as illness or health, sexual behavior, drug use, tax evasion, and other secrets. The more faithfully the researcher upholds the tenet of confidentiality, the more she will "enhance both the quality and validity of data" (Ogden, 2008: 111). Ogden immersed himself in trying to understand the circumstances that might lead people to consider euthanasia (which is an offense under Canadian law). Knowing full well that euthanasia is not a legal option, he had to seriously assure participants that the particular source of data would be treated confidentially.

It is not only in case studies of euthanasia that authorities would try to pressure the researcher to surrender confidentiality. In many jurisdictions, the law demands that the researcher break her promise of confidentiality when she believes other crimes have been committed or a crime is about to be committed.

Third parties (e.g., law-enforcement agencies) do sometimes challenge confidentiality in the hopes of securing identifiable information to "pursue their own non-research interests" (SSHWC, 2007: 6). There is no more perplexing ethical issue than when one's topic or setting of the research seems to conflict with law. Many celebrated studies involve settings that deal with prostitution, drug cultures, euthanasia, pickpockets, ticket scalpers, dumpster diving, motor-bike gangs, and human traffic, and have offered profound insights about such activities. They normally involve thick descriptions of the relevant setting, culture, or group. Qualitative researchers acknowledge the potential for conflict and have therefore devised ways of accommodating themselves to that conflict. Such accommodation, as we shall see below, is not always successful. Is there a way out of this perplexing issue? Yes (for the most part).

The root of the perplexity lies in how researchers are increasingly predefining an area of research in terms of a legal framework. Before research starts, the researcher takes into account that a group or setting is "illegal" and uses that definition of the situation as an inescapable starting point. She will painfully bend the ethical issues of the research around legal requirements. In theory, the world of ethics and that of law are like a Venn diagram: there is some overlap but also areas that stand separately from each other.

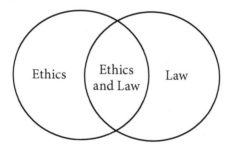

By anticipating and defining a research setting as "illegal," the researcher will have already curtailed the focus of her inquiry within a legal framework. The prevalence of essentially a legal framework within one's research setting can be a disservice to scholarly inquiry as a limiting factor. A scholar is interested in studying the natural real-life world and activities of groups, whether they are legal or not. When a researcher slices that real-life world into "legal" and "illegal," she will inevitably cut off many relevant portions of that group's life somehow as less worthy of scholarly attention. There is much discussion these days about whether law should trump ethics or vice versa. Each university has developed its own sensitivities with regard to the issue.

In terms of the practicality of conducting graduate-level research, a student must attach a moral significance to the legal framework in defining the boundaries of her research. However, researchers do worry that the legal framework may have a deep impact on the lives of research participants despite the promise of confidentiality, anonymity, and privacy. Within those constraints, researchers have found ways to minimize the problems when the legal framework intrudes on research and on the lives of research participants. Criminologists in Australia and Canada, for example, have tried to reconcile the potential conflict between the imposition of a legal framework and the pursuit of ethical research strategies.

In a number of countries there are some buffers between the research participant's promised confidentiality and a third-party's attempts to violate that confidentiality. In Australia, for example, it takes the attorney general to have such parties obtain information gathered for the purpose of "professional or academic purpose" (Israel, 2004: 23). In Canada, the researcher should anticipate the "Wigmore criteria" when confidentiality is essential and when "negative repercussions" would occur to research participants (SSHWC, 2007: 9). These criteria stipulate that communications originating in confidence will not be disclosed. They also aver that "confidentiality must be essential to the full and satisfactory maintenance of the relation between the parties." The Wigmore criteria, however, must also be based on expert testimony that includes "the research community, the community of which participants are members, the social policy communities who seek independent research information for policy formulation and implementation processes, and the broader citizenry, who benefit from the knowledge created through research." Finally, the criteria underscore "the injury as a result of the disclosure of the communications must be greater than the benefit" (Anon., n.d.).

In the United States, a "Confidentiality Certificate" can be issued to researchers. Such a certificate covers a range of behaviors of individuals that, if released, could be "damaging to an individual's financial standing, employability, or reputation in the community" (cited in SSHWC, 2007: 9).

Within the confines of researching an illegally defined setting, a researcher obtains oral, rather than written, consent from the research participants.[4] When the time comes for the researcher to decide whether she would choose either the "ethics first" or the "law first" approach, a researcher of good conscience "may choose one or the other" (SSHWC, 2007: 11). It would, moreover, be unethical for a researcher to commence a research project "knowing that one would disclose identifiable information to authorities," and the researcher should avoid situations where she becomes an informant for authorities (SSHWC, 2007: 12, 14). The impact of mandatory-reporting laws is such that they may hinder research that meets ethical criteria in every other respect (SSHWC, 2007: 14). In other cases, some researchers avoid asking questions that might entail mandatory reporting. Along those lines, the researcher should not be asking questions that entrap the research participants (SSHWC, 2007: 14).

Most recently, a court case involving Boston College played out the issue of "ethics first" or "law first" in a dramatic fashion (Anon., 2012). Decades earlier, researchers had interviewed former members of the Irish Republican Army (IRA) and promised full confidentiality. A federal appeals court, responding to a suit launched by British authorities who are interested in solving murders committed by the IRA, decided that the researchers should not have promised unlimited confidentiality and that confidentiality should be "conditioned on legal approval." In its summation, the appeals court concluded that "The choice to investigate criminal activity belongs to the government and is not subject to veto by academic researchers." Academic freedom, including the right to specify the extent to which confidentiality can be extended to their scholarly findings, is increasingly being vitiated by legal rulings that declare, in some cases, that law comes before ethics.

There is one instance that the researcher might not have any control over, and that is when the research involves "unanticipated heinous discovery" (SSHWC, 2007: 12–13). Except for a small number of "heinous events," the researcher needs to report only on a small number of "events." A research participant's past experience with shoplifting occupies a whole different strand of "heinous" discovery than learning about plans to murder someone.

The mandatory reporting of suspected child abuse is another example where confidentiality of persons who participate in the research can be undone. As Bonnie Leadbeater and Kathleen Glass (2006: 256–257) show, mandatory reporting is a complex ethical matter. Research participants may well have signed a consent form or agreed to be part of the research, but they may not have sufficiently understood the consent as involving the researcher's mandatory reporting of abuse of children. The evidence might be "false, weak, or unsubstantiated." While the researcher may faithfully believe that the evidence is incontestable, authorities and courts may disagree about the strength of evidence. Meanwhile, individuals and families become "entangled in embarrassing or lengthy assessments or legal proceedings" (Leadbeater and Glass, 2006: 256).

For those reasons, researchers resort to anonymously collected information and avoid questions that might reveal this kind of information. Confidentiality, privacy, and anonymity will then be sustained (Yuile et al., 2006; Vaillancourt and Igneski, 2006). A more preventative strategy involves the researcher's meeting with representatives of the agency that receives reports of child abuse to learn more about how and when abuse is reported.[5]

Public and semiprivate life, however, do not always provide exemplary illustrations of how confidentiality plays out. Psychiatrists and practicing psychologists fall at one end of the continuum as upholders of confidentiality. Two doors adorn their offices: a patient can emerge from a consultation without being spotted by a waiting patient who has entered through another door. At the other end, the private life of politicians or reported sex offenders is a matter of public knowledge. On the Internet, Facebook can reveal as much about a person as she allows, and even without such allowance, there are means to extract private information about someone's viewing or purchasing habits. Even with guarantees by researchers, some have challenged the ethical status of researchers' collecting data from Facebook profiles, such as the case of the Harvard University social-network project that decided to aggregately share the collected profiles of 1,700 students. Some scholars "scolded" the researchers for undertaking such a project without the express knowledge of the students, while the researchers claimed that they had taken all possible measures to protect the students' privacy (Parry, 2011).

Other settings also provide an admixture of public knowledge and confidentiality. There are no medical secrets, for example, in clinics run in developing countries. Their limited facilities cannot afford confidentiality. Cultural ideas also drive the extent to which the need for confidentiality is either officially ignored or upheld. In Iceland, all citizens can have access to yearly lists of all their fellow citizens that include income, income-tax paid, social-insurance number, religious affiliation, personal address, and their relationship to the head of household.

There are numerous examples from our daily routines where confidentiality is formally required but constantly violated in practice. When visiting a medical office, the receptionist might ask, in earshot of everyone else in the waiting room, why you need the visit. One of us personally recalled hearing a medical attendant interviewing an older patient in the waiting room, with clipboard in hand, asking about details of that person's private life. Similarly, the curtained walls in a hospital room offer virtually no auditory privacy. With the universal usage of cell phones, everyone has a difficult time ignoring the conversation that is taking place within earshot. When our chiropractor installed the open-space system, all of her patients were routinely directed to occupy an adjustment table amidst other tables where we could easily hear about the ailments of everyone else who happened to be in that space.

As we see, notions of confidentiality are contingent on practices and routines, whether formalized or not. The challenge rests with the researcher to negotiate amidst all of these forms and arrive at a point that serves the ethical paradigm of her research. Throughout this book we discuss the specific challenges a researcher may find in small towns or rural areas, total institutions (prisons, nursing homes), or in age-segregated communities that fly in the face of confidentiality. How can a researcher offset such pressures? Does it make sense to ignore the ethical realities on the ground?

Following Janice Morse (1998: 301), qualitative researchers "cannot and do not maintain confidentiality in the strictest sense of the term." There exist no intermediaries between our research participants and the researcher, and thus the researcher uses actual data. The researcher ends up publishing some of the statements or stories.

The Cloak of Anonymity

Because many of the practices in qualitative research involve personal knowledge about research participants, anonymity is at once impossible and yet very urgent. Most of the data that the qualitative researcher obtains and analyzes come from people already known to her. Unlike biomedical research, there is no opportunity (or desire) to work with charts and so the qualitative researcher is left with the question about what to do with unanonymized data.

In the experience of qualitative researchers, there are research participants who want to have their names cited in the text, in the acknowledgments, and even as coauthors. Based on previous research experience, some participants no longer wish to have their identities hidden (as was the case previously) and wish to have their voice acknowledged in the research.

If there is an urgent need to maintain confidentiality, especially in a small community of interest, a qualitative researcher will need to go to great lengths to foster anonymity. It is not enough to simply change a name. They will need to change other identifiers as well such as age, gender, education, and so on (Morse, 1998: 301). M. D. Khyatt (1992) advocates the use of "discontinuous identities" as a means to more securely protect the anonymity of participants. When the researcher uses more than one quote from a participant, she changes the pseudoidentity among the multiple quotes (see Poulin, 2001, and Gouliquer, 2000, for a more detailed use of this practice).

Full anonymity is difficult to attain in many cases of qualitative research. This research approach often involves face-to-face interactions such as in interviews, focus groups, and field research. Some researchers see analytical benefits in keeping the names of interview participants attached to their transcripts—at least for a while—because it is highly relevant to keep the association of transcripts with the context and attributes of the participant. If a researcher chooses a pseudonym too early in the analytical stage of the research, that pseudonym removes the researcher from the proximity of the research setting, losing personal knowledge of the circumstances of the setting. Should the interaction between the researcher and the participant be analyzed as data, it will be useful to retain the true name of the participant. The researcher must then decide to adopt pseudonyms later in the analytical stage of the research, keeping the real names separate from the pseudonyms, well before publishing the results.

There are some practical problems that haunt efforts to maintain anonymity. It is not at all unusual for researchers to engage in research in rural areas, including villages. When a researcher visits a rural home, word spreads quite rapidly about who was interviewed and on what topic (W. van den Hoonaard, 2003). In Newfoundland outports (rural communities), local residents customarily send their children to the local grocery store when they spot a stranger/visitor in the store. The children's task is to find out more about the visitor and report their findings back to their families.

Other small-scale settings, such as total institutions (prisons and the like), make it difficult to maintain anonymity. Rumors and gossip countervail any attempts at keeping anonymity. Thankfully, a researcher can sometimes rely on the length of time until publication of the study's results,[6] as well as the remote venue of the publications, to guarantee a natural anonymity, but it is not foolproof. The researcher would be taking a dangerous chance by relying on this strategy alone.

Courts can formally challenge the precepts of anonymity. Mario Brajuha conducted fieldwork in a restaurant. When a fire broke out in the restaurant, the police suspected arson and insisted that Brajuha surrender his fieldnotes in March 1983. Because he had promised confidentiality, he refused to release names. What followed were at least two years of legal intrusions that affected his family, friends, and colleagues— and potentially his research participants. He might have saved his family and friends from embarrassment and shame, but he chose to protect his participants at all costs. Eventually, he was able to demonstrate the confidentiality of his fieldnotes and he was freed of any more legal intrusions into his scholarly and family life (Brajuha and Hallowell, 1986).

When a qualitative researcher undertakes historical research involving contemporary people, the question of anonymity becomes more problematic. If the researcher intends to leave her research as a record for future generations and includes oral histories, would the benefit of the research be reduced if she used pseudonyms? And what about the approach taken by the interview participant? What if she still wants to have a pseudonym? Some researchers resolve this problem by allowing the pseudonym to stand until such time when, for example, fifty years have passed, she has surrendered her research papers to an archive. Never obtaining or later removing identifying information (Scott, 2005: 250–251) might constitute a good guarantee of anonymity. However, just because a researcher might not know, or might disguise, who a participant is does not guarantee that the participant will not be recognized by a reader. Nonetheless, this approach might not be an attractive option when the researcher needs to spell out in her publications the demographic, social, cultural, or economic characteristics of the participants.

Anonymity is like a watertight barrel held under water. The pressures that lead to holes in the researcher's efforts to maintain anonymity are always there: the demands to keep one's research records as close as possible to the original setting or interview participant, the exposure in rural areas or small settings, and the need to satisfy the historical record of oral interviews—all can puncture the barrel of anonymity.

Yet the need to preserve the cloak of anonymity is as urgent as ever. As a researcher moves into the study of sensitive topics, of people in vulnerable contexts, and of people who would stand to lose a lot if their names were revealed, the cloak should be inviolable. A researcher must weigh and prioritize the elements of her research, a moral decision that may weigh heavily on her shoulders. Does her research really need to provide detailed background of the research participants? What about dropping the cloak of anonymity of those who are responsible for environmental degradation, persecution of a religious minority, or making life more unbearable for the homeless? Should the cloak be stiffly maintained regardless of the innocence or guilt of the parties involved? In this context, should one provide anonymity to institutions, to villages?

We have found it enormously helpful to discuss problematic issues with colleagues (without revealing any names) and/or to engage in a systematic search through the academic literature to find how others have handled such cases. Janice Morse (1998: 302) recommends some practical ways to conceal the identity of her research participants. She first suggests grouping the identifiers of participants together, including age ranges (rather than specific ages). Second, she proposes that we do not attribute each quotation to a particular participant, "unless there is a compelling reason to do so." She reminds us that a qualitative researcher will have already selected particular quotes as representative of her findings; attaching a quote to an individual (even with a pseudonym) is therefore not necessary. While it is not unusual for the qualitative researcher in her publications to provide a small table listing the characteristics of each research participant, one should be aware that a table linking demographic and other tags might identify persons.

Not all researchers believe that they should cover their research with the cloak of anonymity. Research, they argue, would achieve greater verifiability if anonymity is not maintained. Mitch Duneier, for example, in his groundbreaking (and award-winning) work on New York street vendors of books and magazines—mostly homeless men—decided, after getting permission from the vendors, not to maintain confidentiality or anonymity in *Sidewalk* (2001) except for the one policeman who habitually hauled the stalls and books away from the sidewalk. This approach, Duneier asserts, allows the reader to verify the accuracy and veracity of his data.

Some researchers, however, have taken upon themselves the task of "self-cloaking," namely conducting covert research. Chapter 8 devotes a separate section to both the promise and pitfalls of covert research. Especially in such an approach, the researcher must weigh the methodology and the purpose of the study. Does a study on workplace safety demand a covert approach? How would such an approach fit into an ethical framework?

The Vagaries of Consent

In an ideal world, consent represents a "shared perspective and understanding between researchers and potential participants" about the research (Lakes et al., 2012: 216). In this context, the research participant will have agreed to participate in the research only after fully understanding "the risks, benefits, purpose, and general procedures of the study, as well as provisions for the collection, storage, and use of the data" (Lakes et al., 2012: 216). Following Smythe and Murray (2000: 313),

> [F]ree consent means that individuals voluntarily consent to participate in research and are not induced to do so using any form of undue influence or coercion. Consent is something freely given by the research participant and may be freely withdrawn at any time.

Many ethics codes require the researcher to document consent. They typically insist that consent be obtained in writing although increasingly some notation in one's interview transcripts or fieldnotes or record in the interview transcript will suffice. As social researchers we have an ambivalent view of approaches that highlight individuality. The prescribed consent process reflects the individualism that eschews the social nature of reality—the qualitative researchers' major preoccupation (see also Rivière, 2011: 198). Lakes et al. (2012: 229) describe this "abstract individualism" as one of its limitations. They assert that "the vision is narrow; it ignores historical and social contexts and questions about the purpose of knowledge. By itself, the doctrine of informed consent does not do full justice to the complexity of the ethical judgments field workers confront."

Almost all researchers agree that consent is a process rather than an event. Given the ongoing changes in the research setting, it is unnatural to see the securing of consent as a one-time event. Fieldwork encourages change and growth, and the research participant might need to reaffirm the consent if change is substantial enough to require rethinking

(Wax, 1980: 276). If, however, a researcher demands the participant give her consent too frequently, the process may be needlessly off-putting or annoying to both the research participant and researcher.

If the researcher asks for consent before the (field) research begins, that consent is meaningless because the researcher has not yet sketched out the details of a research plan or even the full purpose of the research (Wax, 1980: 275). There is thus no reasonable basis on which participants can give consent. Janice Morse pointed to this particular dilemma in her editorial, "Does Informed Consent Interfere with Induction?" (Morse, 2008). Ethics committees expect the researcher to fully explain the nature and purpose of the study, but what happens in the case of inductive research that is constantly unfolding in these matters? Morse suggests that we start a conversation with the committee to explain this so-called quandary. The researcher might also want to hint at her research approach while talking with the research participant.

However, there are ways that the researcher can be alert to other potential expressions of consent such as, for example, rendering help to the researcher or being hospitable (Wax, 1980: 294). In the early 1980s, when Murray Wax was thinking about consent in field research, consent forms that required the signature of the participant were viewed with suspicion and mistrust. They have come to be more accepted, although there are many pockets of resistance to using consent forms that require a signature. CEOs, for example, in the experience of some researchers, express a great deal of interest in participating in research, but once the researcher produces a consent form, the CEO summons a lawyer or gatekeeper whose cautious judgment may override the CEO's initial enthusiasm for the research (see e.g., Harvey, 2009: 17).

The consent must be "informed." In qualitative research, the researcher informs participants that she invites them to partake in research, states the purpose of the research and the estimated length of the research (or of the interview itself), assures them that participation is voluntary, and provides a moment to discuss the matter of the extent to which research participants will, or will not, be identified (through anonymity and/or confidentiality). The researcher should also explain if she anticipates any harm for the research participant. Any further discussion about the research should leave the research participant to ask questions, understand how the data will be disseminated, and if there are any risks in participating in the research. The inherent ambiguity of qualitative research, however, heightens the vagaries of informed consent. The research participant may not be fully aware that the very topic of research draws on oppositional groups within the larger study. Bernadette Barton (2011) speaks of a "blurry" consent process because the researcher intends to study other groups while the research participant is "inadvertently" misled to believe that only "his" group is being considered. Would a participant, a Christian fundamentalist, have given consent if he knew that the researcher was also exploring Bible Belt gays (Barton, 2011)? What if the liberatory goals of a researcher's project have the potential of harming her subjects (Barton, 2011)? Would the profiling of the difficulties experienced by a minority serve to uplift or intensify their conditions? A researcher might be reluctant to bring to light prejudices or discrimination within the group if members of that group will be discriminated against by the larger society? Liberatory research will have its consequences, whether positive or negative. The researcher needs to reflect on those consequences for the research to remain ethical.

In a number of ways, qualitative researchers face different issues regarding consent than researchers who use other approaches. For example, the idea of consent being reversible (du Toit, 1980: 283) when the research or topic changes in major ways, might not be applicable because, imbedded in qualitative research, are notions of change. Kakali Bhattacharya's research in India (2007) conveys the shifts in the original content of informed consent forms when emerging friendships with research participants transmute the research into something more personal. The researcher found herself using alternate forms of data collection, such as participant observation, conversations (rather than formal interviews), peer debriefings with people who knew the participant, and photo elicitation. Bhattacharya was exploring how some female Indian graduate students, after having lived in the United States for no more than eighteen months, negotiate their early experiences while undertaking higher education. As it is not uncommon for younger Indian women to look up to other Indian women as "elder sisters," Bhattacharya found herself being liaised as a "sister" to one of her research participants. In that context, the researcher got access to a wider variety of data than she had expected. One of the research participants refused to go over any transcripts with the researcher, "trusting wholly the researcher as her 'elder sister'" (Bhattacharya, 2007: 1111). The researcher–research participant relationship moved away from a formal setting to a much more informal, almost familial, one. This research experience also demonstrates the limitation of the Western model.

Cultural practices and understandings can also disrupt the process of having gained consent. It is not at all clear whether a researched population has consented, for example, to the continued use of the same data in other research endeavors or whether the consent only provides approval for a specific research use. One vivid illustration of this confounding aspect of getting consent involved medical research. When researchers collected blood samples of members of the Havasupai Tribe in Arizona and used these samples beyond intentions spelled out in the original consent, the Havasupais saw "these results . . . as threatening to the cultural and social fabric of the society" (Lakes et al., 2012: 217). One can well imagine how the intentions of a social researcher as articulated in her relationship to a studied group might well be considered by that group as focused on one type of research effort. In this case, less specificity opens up the data-gathering phase to more analytic possibilities as the research progresses.

There is a requirement in some countries, like the United Kingdom, to require qualitative researchers to archive their data. This trend grew out of the ease of storing quantitative data (which can be anonymized without any difficulty), but archiving qualitative data, according to Odette Parry and Natasha S. Mauthner (2004), raises problems. First, ownership of archived data is not a clearly established practice (Parry and Mauthner, 2004: 142) even when taking into account the moral ownership of data by research participants and the economic ownership of the recordings by the researcher. In the end, all relinquish control over deposited data.

Second, given the potential wider use of data by others, it is difficult to know the extent to which sensitive information[7] about individuals will be safeguarded (Parry and Mauthner, 2004: 143). Conceptions of what constitutes "sensitive" data vary across cultures and time. In any event, withdrawing sensitive information would render the data useless.

Third, one would have to agree with Parry and Mauthner (2004: 145) that it will not only be hard to conceal the identity of the research participant but also nigh impossible to hide the identity of the researcher.

Fourth, it is hard for both research participants and the researcher to visualize the long-term aspects of the research. It has become increasingly common for data to be saved for the formal future use by another researcher, but the researcher is not likely to ask research participants about her continued use of the data that might stretch over many years or decades. One could argue that one's qualitative research project is never completed; it involves an ongoing process of reanalyzing data and rethinking theories. The researcher will be hard-pressed to indicate when the research will be "over" and finished. That can be a difficult call to make, but the researcher should be open about both possibilities: the data for some research (such as for a PhD dissertation) might have more natural time limits, while others have a habit of resurfacing much later in the researcher's life. The unanticipated rejection of a book or article can also lead the researcher to return to her data. Under such circumstances, no one would think of seeking "reconsent."

Summary

While confidentiality, anonymity, and consent are keystones in any ethical research, they are complex. Although both private and public spaces regularly see breaches of confidentiality, the social researcher does have an obligation to foster confidentiality as much as possible within the ambit of her research. However, there are many natural aspects of the research enterprise that make it particularly challenging to maintain confidentiality. Typically, many small-scale settings, such as villages or institutions, make it extraordinarily challenging to maintain confidentiality. Moreover, legal authorities can bring pressure to bear on researchers who have investigated "illegal" settings, compelling researchers to surrender confidentiality.

Many researchers, following ethics guidelines, aver that anonymity, like confidentiality, should be part of any ethical program of research, but true anonymity (when the identity and name of the research participant is unknown to the researcher) is virtually impossible in qualitative research. Face-to-face interviews, focus groups, and participant observation make pure anonymity as unlikely as a monarch butterfly in the Arctic tundra. Some researchers believe that anonymity makes it hard to verify the research findings. The need to maintain anonymity may be counterproductive when doing historical research for future generations. Consent, too, is fraught with complications.

Formal consent forms, duly signed by the research participant, seem highly inappropriate in qualitative research, where oral consent will be more than sufficient. The researcher needs to be aware that consent is an ongoing process. However, the process of seeking consent from the same participant at every turn of the research seems very contrived and might undo the natural, good relationship between the researcher and research participant. The researcher must give a lot of thought to the extent to which the research participant shares her understanding of the aims of the research lest there be a misunderstanding. Lawyers and advisers to elites or company executives might frown on consent from executives, despite the executives' own enthusiasm for the research. The changing relationship with research participants may well mean that the nature of consent will change over time. Finally, to allow the research to evolve and develop through the course of the research itself, it is probably best not to be too specific in defining what one imagines the research to be.

Chapter Four

Fieldwork

Because fieldwork, ethnography, and participant observation share characteristics, they also share ethical considerations. According to Nathalie Piquemal (2001: 66), these techniques consist of the researcher's immersing himself in the "daily life of the people . . . [enabling] researchers to get a better understanding of cultural meanings of the group, namely their customs and beliefs."[8]

Fieldwork is enigmatic. John Van Maanen (1988: 2) claims that to do fieldwork requires one to have the instinct of an exile:

> for the fieldworker typically arrives at the place of study without much of an introduction and knowing few people, if any. Fieldworkers . . . learn to move among strangers while holding themselves in readiness for episodes of embarrassment, affection, misfortune, partial or vague revelation, deceit, confusion, isolation, warmth, adventure, fear, concealment, pleasure, surprise, insult, and always possible deportation.

As if these elements do not influence the shaping of ethical decisions in the field enough, researchers also face opposing processes, namely accidents versus plans, numbing routines versus living theater, impulse versus rational choice, mistaken versus spot-on judgments (see Van Maanen, 1988: 2). The diversity of moral cultures in any given fieldwork setting has led Michael Parker (2007: 2254) to say that "the primary moral

---

engagement of fieldwork is the negotiation of different moral complexes with each other. The necessity of living with double standards."

Becoming Acquainted with the Setting

In today's climate of moving research forward as rapidly as possible, there is an inclination to know as much as one can before entering the field. The researcher relies on publications and both formal and informal reports about the setting. Pressures of time, it seems, make it prohibitive to enter a setting without much advance knowledge. Such advance knowledge, however, presents a conundrum on several fronts. First, advance knowledge predisposes the researcher to adopt assumptions, whether theoretical or even methodological, about the setting. In some cases, these assumptions shape the expected findings of the research. This approach vitiates a cardinal rule in qualitative research to prioritize the inductive approach. No less significant are the ethical implications of a stance based on advance knowledge.

In many ways, advance knowledge precludes the stories or accounts of the research participants themselves. This knowledge directs the researcher's gaze to particular areas and perhaps away from others. It deprives the research participants from telling their stories and fully sharing their perspectives. After all, the researcher might inadvertently overlook or ignore the questions and issues that research participants themselves may want to raise. The bravest act would be for the researcher to wait until some data are gathered before delving into the scholarly literature. The researcher cannot fully escape the need to have *some* advance knowledge of the setting, but he should be acutely aware of the fact that such information is speculative.

Piquemal reminds us that the researchers and hosts are from different cultures and therefore "subscribe to different ideas of what can constitute ethical behavior" (Piquemal, 2001: 68). This implies that the researcher must consider ethics from the point of view of the host culture. In the case of some Native communities, for example, there is a body of knowledge or a ceremony that is sacred or spiritual and demands privacy. Nathalie Piquemal, in her research about such a ceremony, was faced with the decision whether or not to destroy her data relevant to that ceremony. An individual research participant had given consent to her recording the ceremony, but the consent was premature. The elders had not wanted her to record any ceremonies. Her decision to erase the tape flowed from her respect for an ethics that required her to recognize and acknowledge the authority of those who knew, namely the elders (Piquemal, 2001: 72).

Piquemal's moral suggestion that we should adopt the ethical perspective of the host culture might not work for all cultures. Qualitative researchers are sometimes engaged in the study of the underside of life (gambling, car thefts, drugs, etc.), and it is hard to visualize adopting the norms of those subcultures. These issues show the importance of being able to reflect on the ethical nature of one's research. A too-detailed template of what ought to be done can work against such reflection.

Gaining Entry

Whether the research setting involves a recognizable collectivity, group, or community or whether the social setting involves an aggregate of individuals (without any significant social bonds), the issue of gaining entry remains paramount.

In the case of collectivities, the process of gaining entry will have a deep impact on one's research findings. When it seems that a collectivity has structured its life around a head, council, or leader, the researcher should feel compelled to approach that head and secure permission before entering the setting. Many communities or groups have gatekeepers, either self-proclaimed or officially recognized. Even in such an ideal situation, matters are not always easily resolved. Let's say the researcher wishes to study a part of the community that represents one of its least desirable aspects (such as violence or abuse). In that case, he will need to be forthright and seek the knowledgeable approval of the gatekeeper. It is customary, however, not to stack one's attempts to get permission with problems or issues that unnecessarily cloud those initial discussions unless there is a clear interest in having them studied. Once a researcher is immersed in the life of the community, its members can judge his intentions and actions in a way that will allow for the development of trust. Such genuine trust allows the researcher to approach issues that were unthinkable upon first entry into the community.

The matter of studying "problematic" issues does not rest with the stay in the field; it has bearings on the dissemination and publication of one's findings. Those findings should reflect the care, trust, and respect developed during one's research.

As it turns out, approaching the official head of a community may simply be a formality. For example, Will van den Hoonaard's research in an Icelandic fishing community 1972) involved initial contact with the *oddvitinn*, the head of the village, who was eager to help in any way he could by arranging for accommodation and providing records and minutes of council meetings and so on, but left Will entirely free to pursue his research goals.

There are also situations where organizations or gatekeepers have no interest in bringing in researchers. One study about Amway shows how the mercantile organization cautioned its distributors to be wary of, and de-identify, people who are trying to "steal your dreams" (Pratt, 2000: 472) and set up relationship barriers through social encapsulation. A graduate student, Sandie Atkins-Idzi (1997), was discouraged from studying the organization and her research interest had to be redirected to studying those who had left, or were ostracized by, the organization. This approach is not atypical when studying closely knit or secretive groups who are sensitive about the way they work, wanting to keep their practices from prying eyes.

Whether the gatekeeper is deeply involved in the details of the research or only summarily so, the researcher's ethical poise is one of learner, prepared to accept whatever the strands of research take him to.

Being on the Inside

Being on the inside of a group one is studying can challenge one's ethical obligations. Sometimes, a researcher has invested so much in the study of, say, an exploited or vulnerable group that he becomes an advocate for that group in the pursuit of justice and equality. Or a field researcher may find himself marrying someone in the group. Thus, loyalties can shift and be quite different from when the research began. Still others would look at a group through a particular lens that would in turn precipitate ethical reflection in a particular dimension. Anthropologist Robert Redfield (e.g., 1971) saw great value in understanding peasant or rural communities in holistic terms and looked for harmony and "what people enjoyed" (Murray, 2005: 62). By contrast, anthropologist Oscar Lewis (1961) believed that a researcher should look for conflicts and troubles (Murray, 2005: 62) in the community. This approach, Lewis reasoned, brings the researcher closer to the life of the community and delivers him from studying an imaginary collectivity, drained of "real" life. Other researchers, however, are less inclined to pursue such a path in the belief that a neutral attitude will more likely encourage research participants to share their stories and accounts.

The ramifications of publishing research sometimes extend beyond the original setting, with enormous ethical implications. Returning to the work of Oscar Lewis, we note the impact of the term "culture of poverty," which some say has unfairly shaped later research on poverty. As Jack L. Roach and Orville R. Gursslin (1967) and others have shown, social researchers have used this concept as a starting point when doing research on poverty-stricken families, lodging their inevitable analysis of poor families in that concept. The "culture of poverty" has left the public and policy makers with "the insistent, culturally determined arguments . . . dominating the discourse in a harsher America" (Isserman, 2012).

Experienced researchers such as Gary Alan Fine (1993) aver that fieldwork inevitably entails compromises with idealized ethical standards. Every occupation, he argues, has an underside that contains secrets or backroom dealings closed to those who are not involved in that work (such as customers, clients, readers of research, etc.).This leads Fine to conclude that the "world is secured in secrets" (1993: 268). It does not take much imagination to think about what happens in the backstage of restaurants (i.e., kitchens) versus the refined appearance of the plates of food set before the patrons. Ethnographic fieldwork is no exception. For the qualitative researcher to remain faithful to being "self-critical, self-conscious, and self-reflective" (1993: 268), he needs to accept the fact that his work involves illusions and deceptive practices, too.

According to Fine (1993: 269), the process of doing fieldwork occurs backstage. The researcher conducts his fieldwork alone, the analysis is private, and actual fieldnotes seldom see the light of day. Even interview transcripts may not find their way into our dissertations, books, or articles.[9] Secrecy is then quite heightened in ethnography, and readers must take a lot on faith alone. Despite weaving a web in the gray zone of secrecy, ethnographers hold on to the ideal of what it means to be ethical. The circumstances of fieldwork slant the researcher away from being the "kindly," "friendly," "honest," "precise," "observant," "unobtrusive," "candid," "chaste," "fair," and "literary" ethnographer. Most of these characterizations explicitly conform to the ideals set in ethics codes. As

Fine asserts, they are partial truths, but the ethnographer believes they are whole truths. Fine enumerates a large number of studies that undercut these ideals, not because the ethnographer is dishonest—far from it—but because social, personal, and physical contingencies continuously invade the ethical realm. Being ethical means being aware that this kind of to-ing and fro-ing can happen, and unless the researcher anticipates this, ethical reflection remains dead wood.

Fine is not alone in his contemplation about ethics in the field. One might go as far as saying that ethnography is morally brittle. Charles Bosk frankly outlines ethnography's "insuperable ethical problems" and its "necessary moral failings" (Bosk, 2001: 200). It's not clear what the antidote might be, except perhaps deep reflection on those problems and failings. The researcher invents a good cover story to access the setting (Bosk, 2001: 203), and there is a long list of ways a researcher manipulates his research. According to Bosk, the ethnographer keeps research questions obscure and vague, does not discuss what the experience of being observed might be like for his subjects, routinely says that the impact is benign, feels little obligation to spell out the research participant's right not to participate, and typically promises confidentiality and anonymity but does not explain or consider how difficult it is to keep them (Bosk, 2001: 204–205). The most fundamental ethical problem is that the ethnographer does not warn his subjects "of the ironic and debunking nature" of his work (Bosk, 2001: 213). The ethnographer's goal is, on one hand, to avoid practicing "empty ethics" (Wiles et al., 2006: 294) while on the other to be cognizant of the ethical dilemmas that in a sense sustain ethnographic research.

Despite these admonitions by Fine and Bosk, Tolich and Fitzgerald (2006: 75, also citing Atkinson, 1990) remind us that as a starting point "qualitative methodology requires the author to stand in the shoes of the informant, and when a research project changes its focus from what was originally approved, ethical pathways could be (and generally should be) written into the work for the reader/interviewee to follow."

Exiting the Field

If staying in the field involves the development of all kinds of relationships that are not so different from those in a researcher's "real" life, it is not difficult to imagine that leaving the field can have a puncturing effect. Those with whom the researcher has developed close and personal relationships might be disappointed by his intended departure from the field while others might be happy to see him go! It's not unlike a guest leaving his hosts' home.

The researcher's exit from the setting should, ideally speaking, express care and mindfulness. For many researchers, the connections may continue on for many years. In the case of Will van den Hoonaard, the contact has remained for some 40 years and counting. Thirty-nine years later, the children (now adults) of one of his key people in the field have even taken up contact with him. Don Handelman and Elliott Leyton, authors of *Bureaucracy and World View* (1978), who explored how bureaucracies handle applications from widows whose husbands had worked and died in a fluorspar mine, reported that many years after they had finished their research, they were given potatoes and the like by the children, now in university, of the families they studied.

No doubt some researchers are elated and relieved to be leaving the field. Hortense Powdermaker, who studied Hollywood, admitted in a retrospective: "As I left Hollywood after a year and drove past a sign marking the boundaries of Los Angeles, I burst into a song, as is my habit when feeling joy. But even that reaction did not make me realize how deeply I hated the place" (Powdermaker, 1967: 225).

Participatory Action Research

In recent decades, participatory action research (PAR) has become one of the fastest-growing approaches in social research.[10] Originating in adult education, international development, and the social sciences (Khanlou and Peter, 2005: 2334), PAR is recognized as a "more inclusive form of inquiry." Participants are directly involved in the research, not as "objects" of interest but where they have "maximum control over all aspects of the research, from conception, design, implementation, data collection, analysis, and reporting of findings" (Jordan, 2008: 601). Action research, community-based participatory research, and participatory research are other forms of PAR. Steve Jordan explains that, historically speaking, several intellectual traditions have shaped PAR, including Marxism, feminism, and post-positivism. Given its challenge to the traditional researcher-and-researched concept of research, it has also meant that the ethical dimensions are entirely new, too.

Following Steve Jordan (2008: 603), PAR is "committed to a politics of equity and social transformation ... that have emerged from a critique of Western social science methodologies." There resides in that stance a host of relevant ethical positions. The ethics framework of PAR exemplifies a commitment to "democratic engagement, transparency and openness, [and] a strong cooperative and communitarian ethos" (Jordan, 2008: 603). To be ethically sound, PAR should have an emancipatory potential (Khanlou and Peter, 2005: 2336). Such a framework shies away from covert research, control by groups outside the group that is being studied, and the funding of research by agencies that have ulterior motives. PAR, according to Malone et al. (2006: 1914), may "challenge institutionalized academic practices and the understandings that inform institutional review board deliberations."

Given the nature of PAR, not wasting the participants' time is an ethical approach worth thinking about. This ethical principle also implies that the research must have social validity from the perspective of the community. Moreover, the beneficiaries of the research should be those who are immediately involved in the research. The strong ethos of PAR implies that researchers should typically study vulnerable and oppressed groups and communities with a view to improving their situation. Researchers should be cognizant of the fact that barriers to participating in the research are ever-present and that they should be removed, whether they involve child care, transportation, time off from work, or other challenges. Physical or other disabilities can also be barriers that must be remediated (Khanlou and Peter, 2005: 2336).

Because the goal of PAR is to release people from "harmful and unjust social structures" (Khanlou and Peter, 2005: 2336, citing Kemmis and McTaggart, 2000), the researcher should be mindful that the research might "unleash serious political consequences" on a vulnerable group (Khanlou and Peter, 2005: 2337). Some (e.g., Cornwall and Jewkes, 1995) remind us that such advocacy may ethically stray into imposing Western cultural imperialism.

Another potential source of ethical conflict resides in the idea that the research process in PAR constitutes a loop of consent, that is, before any major step can be undertaken in the research, the researcher must consult with the community (Khanlou and Peter, 2005: 2337). This process, however, can place the researcher in an awkward position: should he seek approval from the university ethics committee before going to the community, or is it possible to reverse the process to preserve the sanctity of the PAR approach?

If a researcher accepts an invitation to embark on a PAR project, implicit consent is virtually assured because the group has already been involved with the process from the very beginning. The line between researcher and participant is blurred and hard to disentangle (Khanlou and Peter, 2005: 2337). The main ethical principle to bear in mind is that informed consent requires a cooperative, mutual approach; the researcher and research participant have an equal obligation to consider that principle. What needs to be asked is how meaningful is the consent if the research changes over time (Williamson and Prosser, 2002: 589)?

A researcher should be mindful that in groups or communities, individuals may feel group pressure to participate despite their own lack of interest (Khanlou and Peter, 2005: 2338).

Even though the researcher may not yet know what publishing form the findings will take, Janice Morse (1998: 302) believes it is a good idea to spell out to the participant the possibility of publishing the findings and to invite the participant's approval. Researchers can avoid many future problems by discussing this with the research participant at the start of the research (Khanlou and Peter, 2005: 2338; Williamson and Prosser, 2002: 589).

In participatory action research the potential power imbalance between the research participant and the researcher no longer prevails, and thus issues surrounding confidentiality and anonymity play out very differently. The research participants themselves become the author(s)—that is the goal—and the decision whether or not to maintain confidentiality stays in the hands of the research participants.

Summary

Field research is a highly variable process due both to the research settings, which can generate a diversity of moral dilemmas, and to the researcher's ability to work his way through those unexpected dilemmas. To do sound fieldwork, the researcher cannot entertain too many research ideas in advance of entering the social setting. Some fieldwork settings (such as aboriginal communities) require the researcher to closely follow the communities' prescriptive practices. Other settings can challenge the researcher's moral sensibilities. Gaining entry often means that gatekeepers, who must be satisfied, have a lot to say about how the research must proceed. Research participants may not be aware of the debunking nature of some types of social research.

Finally, leaving the field adumbrates some significant ethical issues. What legacy will the researcher leave behind? This chapter also discussed participatory action research, which brings the researcher closer to the community's goals and purpose of the research in the first place.

Chapter Five

Interviews, Autoethnographies, and Focus Groups

Although interviews, autoethnographies, and focus groups do not constitute the whole panoply of methods available to qualitative researchers, they are significantly on the increase and deserve special mention. From the perspective of research-ethics committees, interviews are particularly worrisome: ethics committees prefer "unemotional" interview interactions; qualitative researchers, in contrast, celebrate emotion-laden interviews, whether "positive" or "negative," as a sign of a "successful" interview. Virtue makes a critical difference. As Michele McIntosh and Janice Morse (2009: 102) so profoundly underscore, "[a] morally virtuous person acts for the right reason and with the right emotion. The virtuous researcher is well motivated to commit to caring behavior toward the participant."

Interviews

It is difficult to visualize a more intimate or personal process than conducting an interview. While the setting calls for a code of ethical conduct, it also demands careful shifts in the way ethical obligations are carried out. The extent of prior knowledge of or familiarity with the interview participant plays a relevant role. Typically, long interviews, ranging from one hour to many more, have a "career" contingent on the topic, the

van den Hoonaard, Will C., and Deborah K. van den Hoonaard, "Interviews, Autoethnographies, and Focus Groups," in *Essentials of Thinking Ethically in Qualitative Research*, pp. 51–59. © 2013 Left Coast Press, Inc. All rights reserved.

gender, the emotional or intellectual engagement of the interviewer, or the research participant, and even the setting itself. Other forms of contact, such as chats and conversations, also involve ethical standards.

Conventional ethical standards in interviewing focus on the potential harm for research participants. As Michele McIntosh and Janice M. Morse point out (2009: 81), qualitative interviews do not directly produce physical harm to the interview participant. In rare circumstances a research participant might be harassed or scapegoated for speaking to a researcher. In the opinion of many who have been involved with interview research, ethics committees tend to exaggerate the potential harm that interviews can create. Because members of ethics committees are well intentioned and eager to fall on the side of the interview participant, they tend to imagine the worst, especially if the participant's circumstances warrant special care. McIntosh and Morse point out that ethics committee members use their "moral imaginations" as a basis of their decisions. However, "[s]uch moral imaginings," they further say (2009: 82), "may be inaccurate, unrestrained, and unverifiable." Of the thousands of interviews we know about, there is not one that created trauma or distress. On the contrary, many researchers speak about the benefits that accrue to research participants, who often admit that the researcher is the sole person who has listened to them or provided a sounding board. Whether the story "provoked feelings of deep loss and grief, anger, or despair," Corbin and Morse (2003: 343) report that research participants experience feelings of elation and relief.

Whether informally or formally, the researcher has the obligation to indicate to the interview participant that participation is voluntary she does not have to answer every question, and she can withdraw from the interview at any time. Unless the interview participant suggests otherwise, the researcher intends to maintain the participant's anonymity. However, stating these ethical obligations and rights may prove to be a source of other ethical dilemmas.

First, if the researcher and the research participant are already in a comfortable relationship of knowing each other through other aspects of fieldwork, a statement of these ethical obligations might undercut the bond of trust already established. The interview participant might be surprised if the researcher overtly states these obligations and rights, especially resorting to a more formal manner of address.

Second, the researcher, too, may feel awkward in turning a natural connection into what seems to be a more formal, legalistic approach. The source of this awkwardness stems not from the researcher's personal traits but from knowing what the in-depth interview aims for and that a formal, legalistic approach runs counter to that objective—namely, "to generate data which give an authentic insight into people's experiences" (Silverman, 1993: 91). The formal approach can undercut the researcher's effort to delve into the world of meanings that a research participant wishes to share. The formal consent process can distract the research participant. From the perspective of a qualitative researcher, such awkwardness may well translate into a stilted interview, dissipating the natural feelings engendered through previous contact, and even wasting the interview participant's time.

A more natural approach is for the researcher to indicate to the interview participant that she has prepared an information sheet about the research and her proposal. It is more logical for the researcher to sign such a form (Appendix B provides a sample) than the interview participant, because it is the researcher making the promise, not the interview participant. What's more, potential problems might arise if a researcher were to maintain copies of sheets signed by the interview participant. The potential for inadvertently exposing her name is too great and too dangerous, especially in the case of sensitive topics or where harm is potentially too evident. In those cases, a researcher simply notes down in her fieldnotes that the interview participant has given consent.

An interview, especially a long one, has a "career." As such, the interview may acquire the character of an exchange, a true conversation, where the interview participant might expect the researcher to reveal more about herself than in a short interview. The researcher should not view the narrowing social distance as a breach of ethics. On one hand, the researcher may be the only one with whom the interview participant shares her thoughts and feelings. Deborah van den Hoonaard realized this phenomenon was taking place in her research on older widows (D. van den Hoonaard, 2001). The widows' family and friends no longer wanted to hear about their grieving or their stories. Some widows mentioned that they told van den Hoonaard things they had not shared with anyone else. The research setting provided a safe venue with an interested listener. On the other hand, in such intense or deeply emotional transactions, the researcher should not overstep her boundaries as social researcher; the interview may indeed be therapeutic in the sense that a participant might express deeply felt emotions, but a true therapeutic setting requires a long-term commitment involving someone trained in those matters. Researchers will, according to Smythe and Murray (2000: 331), "hear more than the participant consciously might be comfortable telling them." In most instances, however, the interview setting does not call for a counselor to stand by or be available in case something is amiss.

Cross-gender interviews may generate actual or perceived dilemmas of an ethical nature. When, for example, Will van den Hoonaard (2013) conducted research on women's contributions to cartography, he attended conferences on the subject and felt it was imperative for him to conduct interviews in public settings (such as hotel lobbies) rather than in private rooms to avoid potential misunderstandings. The practical downside included the clatter of noise in lobbies that interfered with the audio recording, as well as the constant interruptions by the cartographers' friends and colleagues who walked into the public interview setting in a hotel. In Deborah van den Hoonaard's research involving widowers, she did not feel the same constraint because the invitation for the interview came from the man in a private home; what was absent was the public perception that the interview space was a hotel room.

The emotional or intellectual engagement of both interviewer and research participant affects the length of the interview. When a researcher first makes arrangements for an interview, it is a courtesy to tell the participant how long she expects the interview to last. Such statements are often guesses, and, depending upon the level of interest on both sides, the interview can be unexpectedly shorter or longer. In the experience of Cherry Russell (1999: 9), interview participants were often reluctant to end the session—not an uncommon experience among qualitative researchers. The researcher should, however, be mindful of the interview participant's time constraints. Ann Oakley (1981) discusses how a woman interviewing another woman can create a mutually understood atmosphere of help. Remember, the researcher can always return for a follow-up interview if it's warranted.

It is important to remember that in-depth interviews do not carry the same risk as clinical trials "that use experimental drugs or treatment that may cause potentially disabling or even lethal side effects" (Corbin and Morse, 2003: 337). Anthropologist Joan Cassell affirms that research participants retain considerable control over the process, and adds that such research represents a "comparatively minimal level of harm" (Cassell, 1980: 31).

A number of researchers, like Avril Maddrell (2009: 22), have long recognized the ethical challenge of how to report interviews.[11] She relates the moments when an interview participant told her some personal details that "they may have been happy to tell me, but not necessarily intended for public consumption." To get around this ambiguity, Maddrell would either double-check with the interview participant or anonymize these kinds of data to render them untraceable to the original participant. Maddrell also decided that it would be fine to cite what an interview participant said about a deceased person, but that she would not cite comments made about a living person. As Maddrell avers, these "ethical dilemmas are everyday occurrences for qualitative researchers" (2009: 22).

Autoethnographies

Much of the research that deals with intimacy requires a sensitive approach, but the ability to carry out such research ethically comes largely from the researcher's own life experience and personal knowledge. It is not something that is amenable to following a set of official ethics guidelines. Still, a researcher will need to become proficient at handling intimate and sensitive issues. This section explores some of the ways that researchers found themselves working with these issues and how they have handled them. We have placed these concerns under autoethnography because that is where the researcher is likely to encounter them. Carolyn Ellis (2007: 12), one of the most experienced autoethnographers and who has produced some of the most insightful thoughts about ethics in research with intimate others, believes that "[a]utoethnographies show people in the process of figuring out what to do, how to live, and what their struggles mean."

Artful complications can also arise when a social scientist becomes bound by marriage and intimate and personal relationships. At Memorial University of Newfoundland (where one of the authors completed a master's degree), it was not uncommon in the 1970s for anthropologists and sociologists to undertake field research in "outport" communities, only to return with fieldnotes and a bride from that community. The potential of such (inadvertent) connections should make it clear to any researcher that there is a near-seamless web of relationships that the researcher must be mindful of, especially when one is doing autoethnographic work.

Ellis's "Telling Secrets, Revealing Lives" (2007) reveals her long-standing research interest in writing about her bonds of love and friendship. She wrote about taking care of her elderly mother, the angry reactions of her friends in her study of a fishing community, the death of her brother, and the loss of her intimate partner, among other things. She can thus shed considerable light on what she calls "relational ethics." Citing other studies (e.g., Guillemin and Gillam, 2004: 264), she wonders how we can deal with the

> reality and practice of changing relationships with our research partici-
> pants over time. If our participants become our friends, what are our
> ethical responsibilities toward them . . . [and] toward intimate others
> who are implicated in the stories we write about ourselves? How can we
> act in a humane, nonexploitative way, while being mindful of our role
> as researchers?

Ellis occupied two split identities—friend and researcher. She betrayed her loyalty as a friend in favor of getting research data. It did not matter that she maintained these identities out of the naiveté of a young researcher. Her "findings" found their way back into the community, "smelling," as she says, "like fish" (Ellis, 2007: 11). The local people recognized all anonymized persons.

Ellis's advice is not a prescriptive list of suggestions. She tells students to "think it through, improvise, to write and rewrite, anticipate and feel its consequences" (Ellis, 2007: 23). She urges them not to believe there are no ethical problems. She suggests that they should make ethical decisions about their research in the same way they do about their personal lives. She encourages them to talk about their research with others. She lets them know that they should be "prepared for new complexities along the way" of their emerging relationships in the field, which grow deeper over time (while some fade away). She suggests that the "process of consent" should always be actively pursued so that participants agree at each new stage of the research. She offers the idea that backup plans are valuable to have, and invites students to include multiple voices and multiple interpretations in their studies. She also cautions researchers not to ask too much of participants who "may get little out of their being part of the study." Moreover, she asks them to think about the greater good of the study: does it justify the potential risk to others? The good must be something greater than for their own good (Ellis, 2007: 23–24).

Nevertheless, one can well anticipate that autoethnographies replete with genuine names may well come to haunt those who participated in the research. It is not known whether the named participants in Carolyn Ellis, Christine Kiesinger, and Lisa Tillmann-Healy's work on bulemic women (1997) had any trouble finding jobs later if prospective employers learned about their bulemic past. Social researchers in the health field are particularly sensitive to any violation of privacy, and that worry extends into the future long after the completion of the research where the researcher has associated individual participants (who have agreed that their true names be mentioned) with diagnosis and identification of symptoms, illness, or disease.

Some academic journals such as *Qualitative Health Research* have decided not to publish autoethnographies. As Janice Morse (2002: 1159) argues, autoethnographies contain information about others "who are, by association, recognizable, even if their names have been changed." For an author to resort to publishing her article under a nom de plume presents other problems, not the least of which is the lack of recognition in her field as an essential part of continuing her work and research. In addition, the personal interest "can overwhelm the study," impeding the theoretical and empirical nature of the research (Morse, 2002: 1159).

Focus Groups

The work of Robert Merton and Patricia Kendall in 1946 laid the basis for the use of focus groups in social research, although market researchers have found them particularly useful (Morgan, 1988: 10, 11). Within twenty years, many researchers found broader applications for the focus group. Herbert Blumer advocated "discussion or resource groups" as a path in developing concepts, whereby such groups would be "discussing collectively their sphere of life and probing into it as they meet one another's disagreements," and thereby would "do more to lift the veils covering the sphere of life than any other device that I know of" (Blumer, 1969: 41).

Focus groups consist of a small number of people, let us say ten, who are brought together by the researcher for drawing out information about topics of selected interest to the researcher, replacing a series of interviews that for lack of time cannot be undertaken. More commonly, they are used in combination with individual interviews "as a kind of validity check" (Berg and Lune, 2012: 165).

The ethical impetus of focus groups resides mainly in those who freely participate in them. The researcher can keep participants' names anonymous and provide confidentiality about their personal identifications, such as occupations and the like. However, there is nothing that prevents focus-group participants from talking about their participation, their opinions about what others in the focus group said, or even the topic of discussion. Moral persuasion by the researcher will go a long way toward solving this dilemma. Out of a sense of honor, focus-group participants are not likely to betray this trust, but some researchers recommend that every member of a focus group sign a statement of confidentiality (Berg and Lune, 2012: 189). This practice will no doubt become more widely exercised in the years ahead. Whether or not participants abide by these agreements will be a subject for future research.

Maintaining Internal Confidentiality

Researchers devote much effort to maintaining confidentiality. As Martin Tolich (2004: 101) points out, confidentiality is "like an iceberg; only the tip is known, but what lurks unseen, below the surface, is also a source of potential harm." What resides beneath the surface is internal confidentiality. When a researcher maintains confidentiality in relation to those who are not part of the research, she speaks of *external confidentiality*. But when the research participants can identify each other, even though pseudonyms are used, then we have a breach of *internal confidentiality*.

We became aware of the challenge of maintaining internal confidentiality when one of our students (Clarke, 2010) was studying the writing habits of professors in our part of the country. Because the academic community consists of a tight network of personal associations, Clarke disguised all of her interview participants by changing their gender, their disciplines, and their home province. Any participant would carry one of two genders and even a different field of study, depending on where they were in the book. Despite all her efforts, we were able to recognize many of them by the particular phrases each was known for! The tighter the group under study, the more difficult it will be to maintain internal confidentiality. As we saw in Chapter 3, rural settings involve similar challenges to achieve promised confidentiality.

Summary

Interviews in the tradition of qualitative research exemplify a heightened sense of trust between the research participant and researcher. As such, the use of formalized and legalistic consent procedures can undercut the purpose of in-depth interviews, namely, to enter into the world of the research participant while embarking on a journey of discovery. Cross-gender interviews may involve particular ethical dimensions. Any "harms" attributed to interview research are, for the most part, minimal. Autoethnographic work takes research to a different place. Intimate and sensitive issues are more likely to visit that kind of research, entailing circumspection. Focus groups resemble an interview setting in some respects. Although participants may feel honor-bound to maintain confidentiality, researchers do resort to confidentiality agreements signed by members of the focus group. Maintaining internal confidentiality is surprisingly hard to achieve.

Chapter Six

Internet Research

This chapter explores a major emerging research trend, namely Internet research. Researchers have taken advantage of the Internet for research since 1999 and possibly even earlier. Part of the challenge is that there is little agreement as researchers try to adapt traditional approaches with varying levels of success.

Mark S. Frankel and Sanyin Siang's workshop report (1999) and the Association of Internet Researchers (2002) constitute the bedrock on which researchers rely to become acquainted with an ethical stance for Internet research. The overwhelming presence of anonymous communication, the global nature and accessibility of the material, and the blurred distinction between private and public spaces (Frankel and Siang, 2002: 51) command the attention of every conscientious researcher.

Despite highly touted public sentiments about the importance of privacy, we are all familiar with ubiquitous everyday practices that entail breaches in privacy. Overhearing private cell-phone conversations, the sharing of private and intimate details over the Internet, the viewing of the personal lives of celebrities and politicians, and "sexting" through cell-phone cameras have all become everyday events. On YouTube alone, there are two hundred thousand three-minute videos, 88 percent of which is new material, often self-revealing the private lives of the featured individuals.[12] In 2011 alone, the pervasive use of Internet media reveals a staggering

van den Hoonaard, Will C., and Deborah K. van den Hoonaard, "Internet Research," in *Essentials of Thinking Ethically in Qualitative Research*, pp. 61–66.

obsession: 555 million websites, 2.1 billion Internet users worldwide, more than 800 million users on Facebook, one trillion video playbacks on You-Tube (140 per person on Earth), and an estimated 100 billion photos on Facebook.[13] Increasingly, according to Paul Rubenstein (2012), individuals use the Internet "to exchange thoughts, feelings, attitudes, opinions, insights, experiences, and perspectives in many different forms including text, images, audio, and video. Social media sites typically use technologies such as blogs, message boards, podcasts, wikis, and blogs."

Here is the rub, as recently posed by *The Stanford Encyclopedia of Philosophy* (2012: 2): "what ethical obligations do researchers have to protect the privacy of subjects engaging in activities in 'public' Internet spaces?" This might lead a researcher to question the stringent ethical codes he needs to abide by. Should the researcher set exemplary standards and not give way to popular abandonment of privacy in many everyday situations? Without the personal practice of maintaining privacy to act as a guide, the researcher is left to worry about ideal standards for the practice of research.

With the phenomenal rise of social media, qualitative researchers were bound to explore the Internet as a source for finding research participants, gathering data, and analyzing findings. As Heather Kitchin avers (2007: 91), it is essential that one carefully categorizes the different approaches inherent in Internet research—such as the extent to which websites, blogs, etc. are open or closed, which require a subscription or can be accessed without subscribing. These approaches vary from highly public and open access to data (much like one would find in a magazine) to highly private sources of data. These categories spell ethical differences in the way the researcher acknowledges the need for privacy, confidentiality, consent, and risk. Researchers also need to think about the extent to which their research on the Internet is intrusive (Kitchin, 2003: 403–406; Kitchin, 2007: 93).

Amy Bruckman (2002: 229–230) has identified various levels of disguising data on the Internet. *No disguise* is required when the participant sees himself as deserving credit for the content. In this case, the researcher can use pseudonyms or real names, but he would omit details (such as unusual personal habits) that might harm the participant. *Light disguise* involves naming the group, but names and other identifying details are changed. The researcher can use verbatim quotes; it is still fine if members of the group can identify the participants. *Moderate disguise* stands between light disguise and heavy disguise. In *heavy disguise,* the research-er does not name individuals and groups and avoids using verbatim quotes if those quotes are searchable. The researcher may also want to introduce some false details. However, given the heavy disguise, the kinds of details that might otherwise prove harmful to the participant can be used.

Some researchers see informed consent as a special problem in online research (Orton-Johnson, 2010: 4). The "transient and ephemeral nature" of many online settings, according to Kate Orton-Johnson (2010: 4), along with unknown large populations, creates problems. Research-ers themselves can adopt "anonymous or pseudonymous identities." It would take considerable effort on the part of the researcher to ascertain not only the true age and gender of the participant but also to verify the offered information.

It is also difficult, according to Orton-Johnson (2010: 6), to differenti-ate what is public and what is private information. There are the material benchmarks (such as paying a membership fee), but there are also the rea-sonable expectations of Internet participants. Major web search engines constantly undermine and change the idea of privacy. The uncertainty of confidentiality, anonymity, and data storage, for example, may lead researchers to believe that choosing to do quantitative research is bet-ter—more trouble-free, ethically speaking—than qualitative research. For example, Kraut et al. (2004: 112) advise us to take particular care when doing research on online support groups. They quote a researcher who mentioned that a member of such a researched group decided not to participate any longer, saying, "When I joined this I thought it would be a *support* group, not a fishbowl for a bunch of guinea pigs."

Publicly available nonintrusive materials on the Internet are not dis-similar to texts and images in magazines. There is a fair expectation on the part of those who post these materials that issues of privacy, confi-dentiality, and anonymity have no currency. There is, in fact, the hope that the posted materials will gain wider dissemination.

However, there is also, as most readers know, another level of online material—the kind that is closed to anyone who does not carry a subscrip-tion or membership to a particular website. Under these circumstances, the website is typically devoted to a cause or a narrow range of topics of self-interest, such as discussion groups involving parents with children who live with a disease or illness. When a researcher enters that particu-lar Internet zone, he will require the consent of all the zone's participants.

(Appendix C offers an example of such a statement of seeking consent in this situation.) Participants in this zone do expect anonymity, confidentiality and privacy. The ethical threshold of gaining admittance to such a zone is particularly high.

Some aspects of researching such zones can be surprising. For example, many websites now carry newspaper editions that require a subscription or fee. It would indeed be quite odd to refrain from using that kind of material for research because of thoughts of privacy, confidentiality, and anonymity. In that case, the subscription or fee is not meant as a way to draw a tight circle around materials but simply a means to generate revenue similar to hard-copy versions.

It is also clear that even if one has gained permission to access the websites, blogs, listservs, or discussion groups that are intended to stay within a tight circle, the researcher must be cognizant of the fact that some online pseudonyms function as personal identifiers (Kraut et al., 2004: 109). Someone who poses himself as "yellowdoor" might indicate a popular, well-known identifier among members of a blog, as personal as the member's own real name. Even the mention of that moniker outside that closed circle is equivalent to betraying a trust, and it should be treated as a real name (Bruckman, 2002: 229). As Ian Convery and Diane Cox (2012: 50) note, research using the Internet must rely on a form of "negotiated ethics," an approach that is grounded in the particular aspects of each specific online community. In other words, much is contingent on each online community's ideas about privacy, boundaries, target audience, and aims (Frankel and Siang, 1999: 52).

Paradoxes prevail when conducting research online. For example, one listserv (about ethics in research) expressed the hope that researchers would use the listserv to conduct research on the topic, yet many posts from members include the notation that their particular emails are intended for private viewing. A researcher would have to consider which expression trumps the other: the personal posting of a member or the general statement of the purpose of the listserv? "The [NCEHR] List Serv is open to Canadian members of Research Ethics Boards (REBs), research administrators, researchers conducting human research and professionals involved in clinical activities in Canada." The listserv adds a note, saying that in terms of confidentiality, "although the List Serv is restricted, it should be considered a public forum. Therefore, authors must abstain from communicating confidential information" (http://ncehr-cnerh.org/en/activities/listserv.html, accessed 15 January 2012).

Another paradox. As a researcher, Will van den Hoonaard is eager to cite his sources of information. But in an earlier work (W. van den Hoonaard, 2001), when the use of the Internet and email for research purposes was not yet clearly articulated, he felt impelled to indicate the particular details of emails he was using to make his argument. To show that these emails were not spurious, he indicated the date, time, subject heading, and text of them. He believed he protected the emailers by first asking their permission to cite their emails (which they gave), and then assigning a pseudonym to guarantee their anonymity. So far so good— except with the Internet's remarkable ability to store everything that was ever emailed, this was an exercise in futility. All the reader of the 2001 article would have to do is to coordinate the date, time, and subject of the email to find the identity of the original emailer.

To offset the Internet's capacity to store every message, the researcher must seek additional ways to offer anonymity of sources. Yes, asking permission from the emailer remains a good practice, but the additional effort would completely omit the date and subject of the email, as well as paraphrase the text in such a way that no Google search can be mounted on its key words. Whether a researcher should go all out with such an approach also depends on whether the original emailer does not mind being completely sourced. The use of a pseudonym affords an initial protection. A reader of the article will have to be Internet-savvy or highly motivated to find the original email. And to what end? The researcher should be inclined, in any case, to couch the original text in a courteous, nonjudgmental tone. Strong security measures mounted on websites, according to Kraut et al. (2004: 113), may actually prevent research participants from taking part in the research.

Research involving chat rooms (and their equivalents) requires special ethical consideration. Contacting the list owner for advice might be the best option because of the diverse and unique nature of each site (Convery and Cox, 2012: 53).

Summary

Conducting research on the Internet is still such a new strategy that its ethical dimensions are not clearly spelled out. The Internet blurs the distinction between the public and private spheres. In many instances, the private lives of individuals are made widely available through either text, audio, or images. Still, researchers ought to think about maintaining ethical codes that are more stringent than the general public assumes when using the Internet. Given the diverse nature of online venues, there are important ethical differences in how researchers should conduct their research. Light, moderate, and heavy disguises, each entailing different levels of identifying research participants, provide proportional protection to research participants. The ephemeral nature of online phenomena has an effect on how researchers make ethical decisions. Some researchers argue that many Internet materials are equivalent to those that appear in magazines and newspapers: they are meant to be widely distributed among the public.

Chapter Seven

Photo Elicitation

The rise of social media and digital photography has reinforced interest among qualitative researchers to incorporate visual materials in their work.[14] The use of these materials reflects a long-standing tradition in qualitative research, and researchers have used photo albums, their own photos, photos or other images taken by research participants, and artwork and images hung on walls in the homes of research participants. Anonymization, as we shall see, represents a core issue in the use of visual images (Wiles et al., 2012: 41).[15]

Sheila Keegan (2008: 619) ascribes two roles in the use of photographs in research. On one hand, these visual materials are a form of gathering data from research participants, whether initiated by the researcher or by the participants. On the other hand, the researcher can use photos to elicit views of research participants. Elicitation techniques can include photo-elicitation interviews (PEIs), in which photographs help participants communicate their ideas and provide researchers the opportunity to ask questions about participants' photographs (Harper, 2002; Hurworth, 2003). They also help to contextualize participants' personal realms in a way that words may not (Clark-Ibañez, 2004). In this way, the photograph acts as both a foil—what Collier and Collier (1986) refer to as the "can-opener effect"—for discussion and a visual depiction of complex ideas that may be difficult to communicate only through words.

van den Hoonaard, Will C., and Deborah K. van den Hoonaard, "Photo Elicitation," in *Essentials of Thinking Ethically in Qualitative Research*, pp. 67–72. © 2013 Left Coast Press, Inc. All rights reserved.

An additional elicitation technique called *photofeedback* has been employed far less broadly; it was used most systematically in 2001 by Alice Sampson-Cordle, a PhD student at the University of Georgia. Instead of conducting full in-person interviews, photofeedback solicits written descriptions of photos from participants, which "can reduce feelings of vulnerability or anxiousness caused by talking directly to a researcher" (Sampson-Cordle, 2001: 44).

Any ethical reflection about the use of photos and images in research that involves research participants entails an extended consideration of both sides, namely the advantages and the disadvantages of anonymity. Ethical challenges diverge on those two approaches alone. Because it is difficult to anonymize images, there might be a need for the researcher to manipulate the images—something that both researchers and participants find undesirable (Wiles et al., 2012: 41).

When photographs are created and/or presented by research participants, the researcher may be forced to acknowledge the possible lack of genuine ownership vested in the photographs. Did the participant really produce the photograph, or did he download it from the Internet or borrow it from a friend or family member? Such derived ownership will cast a rather different gaze or understanding on the particular photograph(s). Does the image still belong to someone else (which could lead to copyright issues)? The next two sections present the arguments against and in favor of anonymity.

Against the Use of Anonymity

Research on children and young people is particularly susceptible to the use of images, partly because of their greater comfort with images (cf. Wiles et al., 2012: 43). One could argue that if there is no name attached to the person in the image and the person is unknown to viewers of the image, the risks are quite low. Face-recognition software (more likely in the hands of authorities), however, might make the potential lack of anonymity problematic (cf. Wiles et al., 2012: 51).

One could also argue that photos and images will acquire historical value over time, whether or not the photographer received consent from the participants. In 2012, the Inuit in Canada's North viewed with considerable interest a recently discovered 1919 film about the Canadian Arctic fur-trading posts and the Inuit way of life. In 1919, the Hudson's Bay Company had commissioned a documentary for its 250th anniversary.

The documentary was long forgotten, but it has now been "painstaking-ly" restored by a film company.[16] Judged by today's terms, the filmmakers did not secure consent to make this film, but it has proved to be a major source of historical knowledge.

Basing their findings on a focus-group study, Wiles et al. (2012: 45) found that researchers can forgo anonymity if the expectations are such that the image creator or poster expects it to be seen publicly. Researchers also reported that research participants were disappointed if they were anonymized in images they were featured in, even if the aim was to elim-inate possible stigmatization. Interestingly, some research participants believed that researchers had no right to change and anonymize the images. Research participants were disturbed to see their faces pixelated or bars placed across their eyes in photos. Research participants thought they were criminalized in the process and were averse to anonymization in this manner (Wiles et al., 2012: 46).

In Favor of Anonymity

Regardless of whether the issues are about copyright or authenticity, the issue of anonymity can present itself as a dilemma. This dilemma is par-ticularly relevant in PhotoVoice studies, which aim at "supporting the active pursuit of social justice through the support of individuals and institutional projects incorporating participant-generated photographs" (Emme, 2008: 624). In these instances, the researcher (and the readers of his research) might have no trouble identifying people, buildings, and places. As Riva Soucie avers in her dissertation (personal communica-tion, 2012), photographs are much more difficult to anonymize than text.

Soucie also points to the perceived ethical problem when research participants post and/or disseminate photographs in such public plac-es as Facebook or a personal blog. This situation is analogous to when participants in a focus group reveal to others what was said in the focus group, or when an interview participant tells everyone that he was interviewed, with the additional unprecedented possibility for a digital photograph to reach hundreds or even thousands of people in seconds online. The researcher can ask participants not to post the photos, but, as Soucie mentions, a researcher has no control over them.

In her study, Soucie asked participants to produce (new) digital photographs specifically for the purpose of the study. Her study used a relatively original combination of participant-produced photographs and photo-elicitation interviews to explore young adults' understandings of the thing they call "home." The results showed that while participants saw their diverse experiences of home as mostly legitimate and meaningful, they had pervasive and middle-class notions of home. These notions center around what the youth term "real homes," which they see as spacious, owner-occupied single-family dwellings built for more or less nuclear families living in suburban neighborhoods. But her research participants often provided her with existing photographs. Some were family photos that participants had already posted on their Facebook pages; another was a photograph of a participant's house that he used in online advertisements for renting rooms in his house (this photo was also posted to Craigslist several times a year). The digital nature of photographs provided the means for such an intense distribution of the images. Significantly, when images fall outside the control of the researcher and when the research participant retains the "original" record of the image, Soucie reminds us that "it disrupts the traditional researcher/participant hierarchy that science (even qualitative social science) is used to" (Soucie, personal communication, 2012). One might think about whether this is a dilemma or a good thing.

Researchers have come up with a few ways to anonymize people in photographs, but not all techniques are satisfactory, especially from the perspective of analysis. One popular way of anonymizing people in photographs is to blur faces or simply place a black line or box across the eyes, or eyes and mouth. One must agree with Soucie when she says that the effect is "incredibly disturbing and it dilutes the photo's affect" (Soucie, personal communication, 2012).

Soucie reminds us of Alice Sampson-Cordle's PhD thesis (2001), which takes another approach called "photo-erase." In published work, she omits photos that are easily identifiable and includes a blank text box in their place. The box serves as a placeholder, a way of recognizing the existence of the photograph and its importance to the analytical insights. For some, this technique is not satisfactory, "because it obfuscates the complexity and richness of visual data (leaving out important empirical data and hiding valuable contexts of the analytical insights emerging from them)" (Soucie, personal communication, 2012). Additionally, and Soucie is the first to make the claim, "there is a risk that important parts of participants' perspectives will be erased" (Soucie, personal communication, 2012).

For the sake of not sacrificing anonymity, and with the permission of her participants, Soucie digitally alters the photographs in a way that makes them more difficult to recognize (e.g., changing hair and clothing, adding or taking weight away, changing colors of houses, removing street signs, etc.). For photos that cannot be effectively altered without losing the intention of the photo (or because the file formats are read-only, making them difficult or impossible to edit), she replaces them with similar stock photos. For each photograph that she presents, she says whether or not it is altered or comes from another stock of photographs. This combination of erasure and modification will, she hopes, help readers get a sense of the rich visual imagery that inspired the analysis while still satisfying the ethics committees and protecting the identities of nonparticipants. Following Wiles et al. (2012b), "it was largely the sharing and dissemination of identifiable images (moving and still photographic images of people and place) that was perceived as presenting the most challenges."

In their research, Wiles et al. (2012a: 47) learned that some researchers shake their camera when taking pictures or blur images. While participants are eager to participate in research and eschew anonymity, they may not always realize the full impact when images are no longer anonymized. The longevity of photographs might heighten the need to anonymize because no one really knows their long-term use and impact. Photos of demonstrators may well lead to arrest and imprisonment, as was the case of a demonstrator in Iran.

Given the complexities with using photos and images in research, Wiles et al. (2012: 49) believe the time has come to place ethical parameters around this type of research. For them, the key issues that each researcher must address are:

1. the status and vulnerability of the research participant *in combination with*

2. the nature of the research, and

3. the ways that visual (and other) data are used and presented (Wiles et al. 2012: 49).

While on the whole there are already so many widely distributed images—many of them quite identifiable—and, according to Wiles et al. (2012: 50), the real risk is quite minimal, researchers should exercise anonymity when the images involve sensitive issues.

Summary

The ethical challenges of using photos in research revolve around the question of anonymity. If the researcher forgoes anonymizing images, photos might acquire historical value. Research respondents themselves might prefer a lack of anonymity and might be disturbed to see their faces pixelated or bars placed across their eyes. To argue in favor of anonymity, the researcher would have to be mindful of the immediate consequences of exposure of the individual. Researchers should consider the research participant's status and vulnerability in combination with the nature of the research and the ways in which visual data are used.

Chapter Eight

Covert Research and Researcher Anonymity

Many see covert research as ethically dubious. But is it? Ethics codes are actually quite silent on the topic, and many confuse deception with covert research. This chapter suggests that covert research not only has a long pedigree in qualitative research, but that it has been (and still is) widely practiced. Many variations mark covert research. Covert research has a functional role in qualitative research either as a means of developing initial thinking about a possible research topic or as a means of starting research. The argument for making covert research ethically viable hinges on a list of criteria.

Ambivalence About Covert Research

The public, ethics codes, and scholars have expressed ambivalence about covert research. As a gut reaction, covert research is something one wants to stay away from. It is not honorable to use people as a means of pursuing one's own hidden research agenda. Yet the public's disdain for and fear of cults in the 1970s, drug users in the 1980s, child abuse in the 1990s, and organ sellers in the 2000s all provide encouragement to researchers to do their research covertly, especially if it involves illegal activities.

More typically, ethics codes in various countries (such as the United States, Canada, and Australia) believe that covert research runs contrary

van den Hoonaard, Will C., and Deborah K. van den Hoonaard, "Covert Research and Researcher Anonymity," in *Essentials of Thinking Ethically in Qualitative Research*, pp. 73–83. © 2013 Left Coast Press, Inc. All rights reserved.

to the principles of respect for people because research participants are not given the opportunity to give free and fully informed consent (Spicker, 2011: 119).

There is surprisingly little in the American and Canadian ethics regulations about covert research. The American Anthropological Association's Statement on Ethnography and Institutional Review Boards, for example, contains no reference to covert research.[17] The regulations of the United States Department of Health and Human Services (2011) embed covert research in a discussion about deception, referring to "observation behind one-way mirror," "undercover observation," and "staged experiment in public place." These notions are a far cry from the way some social researchers understand and practice covert research.

The 1998 Canadian *Tri-Council Policy Statement: Ethical Conduct for Research Involving Humans* (MRC et al., 1998; CIHR et al., 2010) makes only one reference to covert research under a section on "Review of Research in Other Jurisdictions or Countries" (Article 1.12). On one hand, the *Tri-Council Policy Statement* (*TCPS*) indirectly indicates the possibility of doing covert research when it says that "the REB should, therefore, not veto research about authoritarian or dictatorial countries on the grounds that the regime or its agents have not given approval for the research project or have expressed a dislike of the researchers." On the other hand, it disfavors covert research when it states that "[u]niversity research should be open. It is thus unethical for researchers to engage in covert activities for intelligence, police or military purposes under the guise of university research. REBs must disallow any such research" (MRC et al., 1998: Article 1.14).

The revised 2010 *Tri-Council Policy Statement* (*TCPS 2*) explicitly refers to covert research when it says that "researchers will engage in covert non-participant or participant observation and not seek consent" (2010: Article 10.2).[18] At their heart, these statements are not in conflict: they aver the independence of researchers to conduct research regardless of the (dis)approval of particular regimes as well as the importance of not doing covert research on behalf of "intelligence, police or military" agencies. There seems to be no restriction on scholars' doing covert research on their own behalf.

Equally minimalist is the Australian National Statement on Ethical Conduct in Human Research. Australia places covert research under its discussion of "limited disclosure," which "covers a spectrum, from simply not fully disclosing or describing the aims or methods of observational research in public contexts, all the way to actively concealing information and planning deception of participants. Examples along the spectrum include: observation in public spaces of everyday behaviour; covert observation, for example of the hand-washing behaviour of hospital employees" (NHMRC, 2007). The idea of deception remains an ill-defined feature of covert research.

Some scholars have raised objections to covert research. David Calvey (2008: 906), a serious proponent of covert research, reminds us that Robert Homan listed at least eight objections to covert research and averred that covert research flouts the principle of informed consent, erodes personal liberty, betrays trust, pollutes the research environment, produces a negative reputation of social research, discriminates against the defenseless and powerless, damages the behavior or interests of subjects, and/or may become a habit that extends to the life of the researcher. Thus today there is a great deal of reluctance to support covert research, which according to Calvey (2008: 907) is stigmatized.

The stigmatization, however, rests on shaky ground. Conceiving of covert research at a higher level, David Calvey points out that practitioners paint a rather pure, nearly virginal picture of how social research, including qualitative research, is done. This image inadvertently conveys the idea that research is not subject to shifts and that ethical dimensions somehow remain static. Covert research, according to such an idea, is not pure; it pollutes the research enterprise itself. Because research is "messy," the ethical dilemmas are (de)constructed according to contingency. For our purpose, however, we need to ask not whether or not covert research is unethical, but in what manner does ethics play out in any research, including covert research?

Comparing Covert Research and Deception

There is an indisputable confusion between covert research and research that involves "deception" (cf. Spicker, 2011: 118). Table 8.1 highlights their differences, which hinge on participant awareness and anonymity for researcher versus participants.

Awareness by participants. In research that involves deception, research participants know that research is taking place but the true topic of research might only be revealed after the experiment or research. Joan Sieber et al. (1995: 68) aver that "to deceive means to cause a person to

	Covert research	Deception
All research participants are		
a. aware of the research	No	Yes
b. aware of research topic	No	No
Not all research participants are		
a. aware of the research	Yes	No
b. aware of research topic	Yes	No
Anonymity prevails for		
a. research participant	Yes	Yes
b. researcher	Yes	No

Table 8.1

believe something that is not true," and researchers use deception when they cannot obtain valid results by "telling subjects the real purpose of the research." Deception involves lying about the topic of research at least in the initial stages. Typically, research involving deception is used for validating "to achieve random assignment and stimulus control," to "study low-frequency responses," to "obtain valid data without serious risk to participants," and to "obtain information that people cannot validly self-report" (United States Department of Health and Human Services, 2011). In covert research, there are settings in which no research participants are aware that research is taking place and others in which some participants do know about the research while others do not. In covert research, the degree of knowledge about the research can vary greatly, but, to be honest, not all research participants know they are part of research.

Anonymity. At one level, the ethical advantage of deception in research leaves the researcher known to the research participants. That kind of advantage cannot accrue to covert research because in some settings knowledge of the researcher's presence may prove counterproductive. In some settings it is dangerous for research participants if it becomes known that they have shared information with a researcher, or even have been in contact with a researcher. The anonymity of the researcher becomes therefore a keystone for doing ethical research. What is more, covert research can provide anonymity to the whole locale in which the research has taken place.

To define covert research, one must think more deeply about the meaning of deception as a research tool that is commonly used in such fields as psychology. The United States Department of Health and Human Services (2011) is quite explicit that deception "deliberately [involves] misleading communication about the purpose of research and/or the procedures employed in the research." Covert research, by anonymizing the researcher with the potential ease of also anonymizing research participants, whether as individuals or as a group, community, or institution, falls into an entirely different category as a research strategy.

The Normality and Variations of Covert Research

The case for covert research, however, is not that simple. Researchers and university ethics committees have a gut reaction against such research that they need to replace with a thoughtful consideration of the researcher's intentions and the social setting in which the research is to be conducted. As noted earlier, we already have an indication of where covert research might be a possibility, as hinted by the Canadian ethical guidelines (the *TCPS*), when the research involves "authoritarian or dictatorial countries."

For David Calvey (2008: 914) and many other qualitative researchers, covert research represents the "spirit of unfettered, unsponsored inquiry" so ardently advocated in Erving Goffman's Presidential Address to the American Sociological Association in 1982. The promulgation of covert research equates to disruptive thinking in social research, and while not all feel attracted to it, or not all sensitive topics lend themselves to that kind of research, it is not a case of "failed or bad ethics."

Paul Spicker (2011: 118) contends that covert research ought to be understood as "[u]ndeclared, undisclosed research in informal settings . . . as a normal part of academic enquiry." In fact, covert research has a long pedigree in social research. Some of this research achieved notoriety within the ethics community and is regularly used to further the aims of promoting particular research-ethics policies that frown on covert research. Every researcher (and ethics committee) will have to struggle to find a balance between fully informing research participants of the research or choosing the path of complete anonymity. These are difficult choices, but one must also consider the fact that it is not always possible to fully inform participants about the proposed research and that virtually every research undertaking has a covert aspect to it (as we shall see later). Thus, in some cases the choices might be not too far off from each other.

One might indeed conclude that some covert research projects were the principal triggers in formalizing a code of research ethics. Leon Festinger's 1956 study of a doomsday cult and Laud Humphreys's 1970 work on homosexual behavior in public restrooms occurred before formal ethics codes became the norm. No less famous was Howard Griffin's study, *Black Like Me* (1977), where he took tablets to darken his skin so that he could easily move among the black population in the southern United States and record the prejudice and discrimination experienced by black people.

Calvey (2008: 909) shows that covert research has a long tradition[19] involving studies of Alcoholics Anonymous, mental-health hospitals, juvenile gangs, Scientology, pilfering by bread salesmen, Pentecostals, extreme right-wing organizations, police, schools, Ku Klux Klan, cannabis dealers, courtships, bouncers, organ traffickers, and lying in the workplace. For *The Rebels* (1991), Daniel R. Wolf rode with outlaw bikers for three years before informing them he was doing research. Timothy Diamond, in *Making Gray Gold* (1992), studied five for-profit nursing homes after having trained as a nursing assistant for the purpose of his research. The management never knew of his presence as a researcher, although Diamond did not hesitate to explain his role as a researcher to front-line staff (who wished him luck). As far as we can reckon, anonymity was preserved completely, and neither the groups nor individuals suffered from the research.

When a researcher is watching a parade or a crowd for research purposes, or watching to see if drivers are using a cell phone or rolling through a stop sign, he is carrying out covert observation. Covert research covers a large spectrum of research activities (Spicker, 2011: 119). Some overt research might have covert elements, and some covert research may be known to some research participants but not to others. Covert research runs deeper than the above examples. One might say that, almost without exception, every qualitative research project has either an intended or unintended covert element to it.

The idea of doing covert research does not necessarily cover all parts or all participants in research. In Marco Marzano's study of a large Italian hospital (2007), for example, the medical staff knew of his research intentions, but the patients did not. Eventually, the covert cover was fully pulled back. Even research without the intent of being covert has covert elements, and these elements have a functional place in qualitative research.

Functional Place of Covert Research

Even before the research formally starts, a researcher will take notes of particular settings either to see whether research would be feasible or simply because he has a personal interest in a setting (which may then lead to research). These musings are critical to research, for they fine-tune one's early observations and early reflections. It is virtually impossible not to use "covert" research as part of the early-musings (or exploratory) stage of research.[20] For example, our own (unpublished) work on airports started with our musings as avid travelers forced to spend time in airports about behavior in airports. Will van den Hoonaard's first book, *Silent Ethnicity: The Dutch of New Brunswick* (1991), probably started with informal discussions with Dutch-Canadian farmers at a farmers' market. Similarly, Deborah van den Hoonaard's research on retirement communities began with visits to her parents before she had contemplated graduate work on that topic while taking some early research notes about the retirement community. Were they doing covert research?

Some of these initial notes may not find their way into research projects or publications; others, however, will germinate into full-scale research projects, because the fascination stays with the researcher. Those early notes in the development of research are comparable to the crawling stage of infants before they take their first upright steps. Crawling cannot be discounted; nor can one's early field-note musings. In this vein, some incipient researchers are highly organized in note-taking; others are less so. But their foundation is the same: fascination with the social processes before becoming fully engaged in doing research.

But here is the conundrum: does a researcher need to secure post hoc research-ethics approval for those initial musings? Or is such approval out of the question? So far, experience dictates that ethics committees are loathe to grant such post hoc approval. If no approval is forthcoming, is the researcher's choice to continue this fascination as a research project taken away because he did not conceive of it as "research" ahead of time and get the requisite approval, just in case?[21] Can a researcher ever unknow what he has noticed and thought about?

Covert research also plays a critical role once the research starts. The formal entry points of countless research projects happen along those lines. We use the term "happen" advisedly, because ethnographic or qualitative researchers are in the habit of taking fieldnotes as soon as they find themselves in the research setting. Those early note-taking practices embed an understanding that is not yet tainted by the everyday, taken-for-granted world of the setting that the researcher has embarked on. In the tradition of social-scientific work (argued persuasively by C. Wright Mills [1976]), note-taking as a means to further one's reflection and understanding of events is a critical aspect of such work. Gans's classic study of the Levittowners (1967) started when he and his wife bought a house in Levittown, and he immediately began taking notes on the social interactions among neighbors, newcomers, and local rural residents. It is quite impossible to conduct good research without resorting to creating and analyzing fieldnotes of those early experiences, sometimes long before the first research participants are met. As Erving Goffman assured us, these early notes are critically important to write down: "The first day you'll see more than you'll ever see again. And you'll see things that you won't see again. So, the first day, you should take notes all the time" (Goffman, 2004: 152).

Similarly, in interview settings, a good qualitative researcher sees great value in taking notes and will not hesitate to do so. Could one say that this is covert research? Common sense tells us that this is a normal practice when doing qualitative research.

Aside from those musings, early fieldnotes, and notes about interview settings as a form of covert research, there are other layers of research that could be construed as covert. Once we acknowledge the existence of these layers, we start to realize that many of the conventional objections to so-called covert research fall away. Take informed consent as an example of one "covert" layer. Even under normal circumstances, when a qualitative researcher tries to explain the research project, he is not (yet) in a position to explain to the research participant the project in full. He has no choice but to couch the explanation in generalities because the specific aspects of the research can only emerge over time. One could interpret his partial explanations as partial truths and, therefore, part of "covert" research. A researcher is unlikely later to share a change in the purposes of the research, even a substantial one, with the research participants. Nor will he likely let the participant know who is paying for the research (Thorne, 1980: 287–288).

Criteria for Conducting Covert Research

Taking our argument to a more practical level, we note that social researchers have often researched collectivities, whether as communities, religious groups including cults (e.g., Lofland, 1966), self-help groups (Davis, 1960), or ethnic or aboriginal groups. What are the criteria for deciding on doing covert research? What if the leadership of a collectivity decides that a given setting under its jurisdiction should not be investigated? What if that setting involves injustice, violence, etc.? Does the leadership have the right to deny access to that setting and, therefore, the right of its members to participate in research? Would the researcher have the moral right (or duty) to conduct research anyway, even if it is covert? Does the status of covert research change radically if the group has been historically disadvantaged or persecuted? Is covert research the last thing one wants?

What about research on corporations? To our knowledge, very few corporations allow academic research, even as non-covert research. (Among the exceptions are the corporations studied by Arlie R. Hochschild and reported in her 1997 book, *The Time Bind,* and Rosabeth Moss Kanter's *The Men and Women of the Corporation* [1977].) Libel, lawsuits, the inevitable fall of whistle-blowers, and the power of multinationals are enough of a disincentive to conduct any kind of research in those settings. Will it be sufficient, for example, to interview ex-employees? Is that a fair approach to the study of a corporation?

Increasingly, cultural groups completely reject the idea of covert research: they want to review the research and negotiate conditions, and sometimes refuse to be studied at all (Thorne, 1980: 284). Such rejection is understandable given the negative impact that internal colonialism has had on the portrayal of ethnic, cultural, or aboriginal groups.

It is very important to weigh factors that impinge on the decision to undertake covert research, including the status of the group or social setting being researched and the importance of the research. Nancy Scheper-Hughes, a professor of anthropology at the University of California, Berkeley, provides an illuminating example of covert research. Known for her writing on the anthropology of the body, she found herself wanting to research an international ring of organ sellers based in New York, New Jersey, and Israel (Scheper-Hughes, 2002). The only manner to conduct the research was covertly. As a way of introducing herself to the smugglers of organs, she put out the story that she wanted a new organ for her mother.

We can learn a few lessons from the hymn book of covert research, namely that "[d]isclosure and impartiality are more complex than assumed by ethical codes" (Aldred, 2008: 896). The conditions of covert research preclude consent by research participants and can protect both research participants (by not revealing the locale of the research) and researchers from harm. It should only be used in a research setting where "open and transparent research is impossible" (Aldred, 2008: 896). Moreover, because covert research is suspect, those who engage in it may actually think more deeply about its ethical implications.

An Illustration of Covert Research

David Calvey's research (2008: 910) on nightclub bouncers in Manchester, England, suggests ways that covert research can be carried out. His research was part of a study of the nighttime economy in which various agencies are professionalizing the bouncer trade. That time period attracted Calvey's special interest: the agencies were trying to pull bouncers out of the shadow economy and demonstrate their connection to criminality. His goal was to get an accurate and authentic picture of a closed world that aroused "both fear and fascination" (Calvey, 2008: 911). To carry out his work, he became city-certified as a doorman. It helped that he had been trained in the martial arts. In due course, he would "retire" from the door community but would meet doormen at clubs. He informed them that he was now retired and "couldn't stand the pace anymore."

The most challenging part for Calvey was the personal, uneven relations between him as researcher and the doormen: he could not explain parts of the relations that he had often to gloss over (Calvey, 2008: 911). He felt he was getting close to them without their getting close to him. He provided as little personal information as he could. Moreover, because he could not limit himself to one door—he was studying a culture, after all—he had to invent reasons for leaving one door for another.

The greatest challenge by far for Calvey was the "blurred self" of the researcher (Calvey, 2008: 913), that is, an identity that involved a partial self-abnegation in order to assimilate to his setting. He therefore refused to be a moral guardian or an "academic zookeeper" (Calvey, 2008: 913). He had become a credible member of the door community—which pleased him—but he also had nagging thoughts about what he had learned about drug taking, violence, the role of police, and cuts from door money. He had acquired deviant knowledge, but he was engaged in a type of "fingers crossed ethnography" (Calvey, 2008: 913). Calvey exercised moral caution when he turned the tape recorder off when a bouncer told him about private family matters. The moral panic instigated by local press (front page of the *Manchester Evening News*) complicated the issues of the postfieldwork self when he was recognized on several occasions by doormen he used to work with and had to go temporarily back into character and feign that he had retired (email from Calvey to authors, 7 September 2012).

The answer to the dilemma of doing covert research does not lie in banning it altogether. Rather, it involves recognizing that many complex factors are at play, such as the status of the group that is being researched and the need to establish extreme anonymity. One must realize that covert research is the only absolute guarantee of anonymity (W. van den Hoonaard, 2003). Any published report from the research cannot be traced back to the researched group. While in quantitative research it is relatively easy to foster anonymity by stripping away any identifiable information from data sets, it is sometimes quite impossible to guarantee anonymity in ethnographic or qualitative research .

Summary

Covert research, despite its relevance and importance, is seen as ethically dubious. Ethics codes and guidelines are generally silent about covert research. They also conflate covert research with research using deception, despite their incompatible meanings and uses. Covert research is thought to be contrary to the principles of respect for people because research participants are not given the opportunity to give free and fully informed consent. Virtually all social research, including qualitative research, shows that covert research does take place, to a lesser or higher degree. At one extreme, researchers in authoritarian or dictatorial countries or those researching illegal drug cultures typically engage in covert research. At the less extreme edge, when researchers gather preliminary information about possible research settings before engaging in formal research, they are also doing covert research. Similarly, the earliest aspects of research include taking fieldnotes, which is engaged in covertly. This chapter sets out a number of criteria by which covert research can be practiced and provides an illustration from an actual research project by David Calvey that shows how he safeguarded the ethical dimensions in his research.

Chapter Nine

People in Vulnerable Contexts

Historically, qualitative researchers have had a long-standing interest in conducting research on, or with, people in vulnerable and marginal contexts. Many see the inductive nature of qualitative research as ideally suited for undertaking this kind of research. Qualitative researchers have a nose for not pandering to prevailing public or policy-oriented views or solutions. This stance makes them eminently suitable to research groups who have fallen beyond the ken of mainstream society, such as those who are homeless or elderly. In a real sense, the qualitative researcher believes she can make a special contribution to understanding and analyzing people in these contexts given her tools of the trade. What always stands out for a researcher is the vital need to be aware that powerless social groups require more protection than the powerful, who, as Cloke et al. (2000: 135) aver, "are able to protect themselves." The researcher often attempts to provide a "voice" to those who have been rendered voiceless or silent by society.

Typically, many speak of *vulnerable, marginal,* and *disabled* people, but such shorthand characterizations are not up to the task of describing what the research should be about. We discover, for example, that the term *vulnerable people* downplays the fact that they are often hardier than one initially suspects. Some are towers of strength and resilience but lead their lives in a context that could make them vulnerable. The characterization of people as "vulnerable" extends a stereotype that extinguishes

van den Hoonaard, Will C., and Deborah K. van den Hoonaard, "People in Vulnerable Contexts," in *Essentials of Thinking Ethically in Qualitative Research*, pp. 85–94.

the vestige of human dignity. It is a tempting stereotype because it sweeps all differences under the carpet. Our inner ethical poise as researchers insists that we avoid this stereotype, which will in due course penetrate into our analysis. The term *vulnerable people* is a misnomer. One knows of too many instances where, for example, a street kid demonstrates a lot of street smarts to survive the rigors of being in a vulnerable context. We see a "bag lady" in New York's Grand Central Terminal who manages to defend her territory of receptacles from intruders and provide her own sustenance. On a grander scale, one sees someone achieve acts of heroism under the most trying circumstances. The vulnerable context remains, but in that same context, some survive just barely, others become masters of their circumstances, and others fall in between those two extremes.

The above observations are no less true for so-called marginal people. If one remembers that the coinage of such a term comes from the "center" of things, it is not hard to realize that "marginal" might be quite off the mark: some people on the "margins" may not feel that way at all, and others would readily acknowledge they are on the margins but are quite happy to be there. Being on the margins has no objective reality, and the researcher has an ethical obligation to treat those margins as such: they are social constructs.

People with disabilities would, according to the growing body of literature on the topic, agree with many of the above sentiments. It has become common knowledge that when one speaks of "disabled people," important parts of their lives are left out of the equation. There are not only many identities attached to people with disabilities but often the characterization of someone as disabled gets frozen in the eye of the gazer. In other words, if a researcher funnels all of her analysis along the "disabled" spectrum, her analysis will be poor indeed. Hence the desire of disability studies to focus on how society makes people disabled.

The special ethical challenge for the researcher is to escape the entanglement of taking things for granted, if only because a researcher often lives in a nonvulnerable and nonmarginal context. Not being disabled provides yet another ethical dilemma for a researcher when doing serious research on people in vulnerable contexts.

Vulnerable Contexts

Today's ethos embraces such terms as *vulnerability* and *resilience* and the like. Not only are these terms empirically abstract (i.e., they do not take into account the many dimensions of vulnerability), they reflect individualism. These abstract and individualistic terms pose a problem for qualitative researchers who are more inclined to see social patterns. When we introduce the term *context*, we recognize social reality and that individuals are contingent on the larger social framework. This particular approach is so very evident in Elliot Liebow's classic study of homeless women, *Tell Them Whom I Am* (1993). Liebow had spent most of his anthropological life as a civil servant until he was diagnosed with terminal cancer. He then set out to do what he loved the most, ethnographic research, and produced a wonderful study of the situation of homeless women. The study represents the kind of deep ethical research that one hopes to achieve.

Doing research on people in vulnerable contexts should lead the researcher to think about Timothy Diamond's relevant advice (1992: 84–85) when he reflected on his research on the life of staff and residents in for-profit nursing homes. The researcher needs to transform her questions from "what can we do for them?" to "what is it that they are doing?" The former question "contains within it the seeds of reinventing passivity" on the part of the residents; the second question indicates a belief that residents are agents rather than "objects of action." The second question also leads the researcher to ask "what kind of human activity does it take to live in a nursing home?" The reader can sense a fundamental shift of perspective from the first to the second question, namely from trying to solve the "problem" to fully understanding the world inhabited by the residents. The researcher should deeply self-examine the vestiges of her own prejudices before tackling research involving people in vulnerable contexts. Above all, the researcher should forgo a "remedial" attitude.

The study of people in a vulnerable context may generate a complex moral decision. The researcher may well confront a situation that involves abuse or exploitation. The easiest "remedy" is to report the incident to those responsible for its correction. One's moral center will be reaffirmed. But is such reporting the most appropriate moral choice? Individual research settings vary enormously, but if the setting involves an institution or organization, the researcher will need to ask herself whether her attempts to report the incident immediately will, in the long run, prove helpful. If abuse or exploitation is inherent in the situation, the researcher may decide to continue the research and, at the end, provide evidence that the abuse or exploitation was endemic, and, we hope, the pattern of abuse will be entirely halted or officially investigated. In contrast, if the researcher immediately reports an instance of abuse, it means that her research will be halted and access to the setting will be closed off, maybe even permanently, allowing the pattern of abuse to continue. One further consideration: might not such reporting put the victim of the abuse into further danger?

While part of the decision rests on the belief that an immediate response relies on one's moral sense, the other side relates to fundamental assumptions about the nature and goal of social research. Social research involves the discovery of systemic patterns of interaction; an immediate attempt to stop the abuse brings the social research—and the long-term solution—to a vivid halt.

Children

Research with children continues to be one of the most challenging issues in qualitative research, despite the fact that it represents a physically less harmful way of conducting research than clinical trials. Ethical decision making turns on the question of assent or consent and the nature of the topic one is researching.

One finds wide discrepancies in the way researchers, schools, parents, and agencies approach research with children (Leadbeater and Glass, 2006: 251). The problems that Melissa Swauger sketches are not uncommon in ethical research involving children:

> I intended to build rapport and trust among the potential participants and use our interactions to frame my focus group and interview questions. However, the [ethics committee] denied my proposal to observe girls until I had parents' consent. Later, when recruiting girls for focus groups and interviews, I learned that some potential participants were in foster care and that I could only include these girls if I obtained consent from a biological parent. I, along with caseworkers at the organization, found it ethically questionable to attempt to locate a biological parent of foster girls because many parents were inaccessible. Gaining biological parental consent proved especially uncomfortable during the interview stages of my research when a girl in foster care asked me why I did not ask her to participate in the study. I had to tell her that I had to exclude foster children. (Swauger, 2011: 497)

This book cannot do justice to all of these dilemmas in the diversity of approaches in researching children. Some schools (and principals) allow for a waiver of written parental consent as long as the parents have been informed (Leadbeater and Glass, 2006: 251), while others require signed parental consent. There are also situations when parents agree with the waiving of signed consent, but there is among aboriginal parents the requirement that no research be allowed unless they have given explicit consent. Often, the formal and informal guidelines about research on children vary considerably among university bodies, school organizations, parents, and communities, which puts the researcher in a quandary. Moreover, journal editors and peer reviewers may have set their own requirements about publishing research involving children.

The topic of the research also enters into any consideration about the ethical nature of research on children. When a researcher explores the sexual behavior or interests of children, would the impact of parental consent jeopardize children? What about gambling and illegal activities (vandalism, graffiti on public buildings, etc.)? Should one discourage such research because the process of consent would endanger the child, even though such research can contribute to the overall welfare of society?

The age and maturity of the child is an important consideration in the matter of gaining assent and/or consent for research. This distinction gains significance as the child becomes an adolescent. There is a wide range of age-related distinctions when one thinks of the drinking age, the right to vote, the right to have a driver's license, the right (or the legal compulsion) to attend or leave school, the right to receive social welfare, the right to join the military, and so on. The legal requirements related to the age of children do not leave much room to pay attention to the distinctive ethical needs of research on children.

In any case, the idea of "maturity" has become quite relevant when deciding about the age of consent for a child (and whether the researcher also needs the consent of the parent). Everyone who has met children (of any age) knows too well that some children appear to be more mature than their age peers. As a consequence, this difference in maturity would spell a different approach. Obviously, it will be hard for any researcher to pick an age of consent. The Canadian ethical guidelines on research do not specify an age of consent for children (PRE, 2011):

> but on whether they have the capacity to understand the significance of the research and the implications of the risk and benefits to themselves. . . . Factors to consider in making the decision to seek consent from children as participants include, but are not limited to, the nature of the research, the research setting, the level of risk the research may pose to participants, provincial legislation and other applicable legal and regulatory requirements related to legal age of consent, and the characteristics of the intended research participants—who may differ

in many aspects including their competence/cognitive capacity to make their own decisions. As no two research studies or research participants are identical, the decision to seek consent from children instead of an authorized third party should be considered on a case-by-case basis. In practice, the researcher plays a key role, sometimes in association with the parents, in determining whether the child is able to consent.

Children who lack capacity to consent may still be able to express their wishes in a meaningful way (assent or dissent), even if such expression may not be sufficient to fulfill the requirements for consent. Researchers must respect the decision of children who are capable of verbally or physically assenting to, or dissenting from, participation in research, even if the authorized third party has consented on their behalf.

It will be critical for the researcher to be able to figure out the appropriate age for the child to consent (or not) to do the research.

Conducting research on children through the Internet requires additional layers of assurances. Given the possibility of masking one's age, some researchers want an assurance that a particular participant is a child and that a parent has agreed to the research. A number of national and subnational jurisdictions require the researcher to post a notice about how the information will be used (Kraut et al., 2004: 114).

Inmates

The restricted circumstances faced by inmates of prisons, nursing homes, and hospitals constitute their contextual vulnerability. Any research that explores the world of the administrators and/or of its inhabitants (i.e., inmates) can unintentionally produce a dynamic that could shape and redirect the social arrangements within the institution. It is the inmates who are likely to incur the negative impact of these changes, rather than the administrators.

Typically, research on inmates (and administrators) produces a desire on the part of researchers to see their work as an attempt to remedy a situation. Such a stance precludes the possibility of conducting ethical research because the researcher is already committed to a position. The line of authority drawn between administrators and inmates produces difficulties when one group is seeking information about the other. As a consequence, the researcher should not allow himself to be a purveyor of that information. While another strand of research, namely participatory action research (PAR), also attempts to remedy situations from the perspective of research participants, it does not do so with the express aim of purveying information to those inimical to the perceived interests of the research participants.

A researcher ought to withhold any promise to any inmate, whether it relates to early release, preferential treatment by staff, or arrangements for family visits. As it is already difficult (and precarious) to maintain confidentiality and anonymity in such research, it will take extra effort to guarantee them.

The researcher should understand that administrators and staff may have a naive view of social research and see no problem in the researcher's surrendering detailed information to them. They may take it for granted or insist on identifying interview participants.

The experience of inmates is such that their behavior is always scrutinized. The arrival of a researcher from outside the institution does not change their view of scrutiny. The researcher is confronted with two nearly unresolvable challenges. On one hand, there is the potential distrust of the inmate, who sees the researcher as an agent of the institution. On the other hand, the institution has no true understanding of what it means to have research undertaken independently of the needs of the institution. Thus, a researcher may find herself in a situation where she cannot guarantee full confidentiality but can only offer limited confidentiality.

As an illustrative example of how studies with limited confidentiality can yield worthless results, we refer to a study by Ivan Zinger and Cherami Wichmann (1999), which found "few negative effects resulting from long-term segregation" (Wichmann and Taylor, 2004: ii). As Ted Palys and John Lowman (2001) have shown, it was the limited confidentiality that prevented inmates from revealing any negative aspects of their confinement. Palys and Lowman cite the statement the original researchers, Zinger and Wichmann (1999), read to the inmates-cum-interview participants:

> Before we begin, I need to tell you that although the information you provide today will be confidential, there are limits. I have an obligation to disclose any information you may provide if it's in regards to your safety or that of the institution. These areas include suicide plans, plans of escape, injury to others and the general security of the institution. (Zinger and Wichmann, 1999: 107)

Regardless of the reporting obligations, it is clear that no inmate was inclined to give much detailed information.

Mark Israel (2004: 23–24) reminds us that "when a researcher comes into possession of information about offences being committed [by the research participant]," it might be hard for her to decide the proper course of action. It is too complex. He shows that when a researcher reports criminal activity, the police normally require a higher standard of proof. Vague, old, or unsupported information will not suffice. In some cases, reports to the police may not be in the best interest of the participant, who might be placed at an even greater risk (Israel, 2004: 24).

On the Margins

Being on the margins can involve social, economic, or geographical designation, and can represent a formidable challenge to any researcher who wants to come to terms with doing such research. The greatest challenge faces the researcher who does not come from the margins, for she brings concepts and approaches into her research that differ widely from those current among people on the margins. Aside from entering an unknown world of people, a researcher most probably faces "the demystifying experience of explaining the validity of [her] research to those in need," resulting in "considerable ethical turbulence" (Cloke et al., 2000: 139) involving competing ethical obligations. The core ethical challenge is thus researching the "other" (Cloke et al., 2000: 132). As Cloke et al. (2000: 135) remind us, "it is commonplace to distinguish between research on powerless social groups—where rights to privacy and protection are very important—and research on the powerful, who are able to protect themselves."

Doing qualitative research on marginal groups indeed generates "thick descriptions," but such an approach raises more difficulties than "more quantitative strategies in maintaining the confidentiality and privacy of those with a personal involvement with the research" (Cloke et al., 2000: 135).

Some researchers, like Ingeborg Helgeland (2005: 563), believe that the social good obtained by researching marginal groups clearly outweighs the disadvantages. Members of marginal groups "liked getting chances to speak their minds and [discovering] that someone was interested in listening to their experiences.... If they had been protected against being brought into the study, their voices as independent actors would have never been heard."

People on the margins have learned to build bridges to the center. Such an approach is either absent or negligible when trying to reach the margins from the center, and such differences translate themselves unsuspectedly into ethical dilemmas that can undermine one's research.

People with Disabilities

Will van den Hoonaard found himself in the situation of interviewing a near-ninety-year old woman who, not too long before the interview, had had a stroke. Her whole left side was paralyzed. Once she heard about the research, she wanted to participate, and the researcher, in light of her historical knowledge, gratefully accepted the invitation. After the conversation/interview had progressed for about an hour, the researcher asked the woman whether this was a good time to take a break. He was getting fatigued. The woman, however, replied that she believed it was not a good time to stop. She was on a roll . . . and was not tired.

Underestimating the power of people with physical disabilities must be a common situation for researchers to find themselves in. Part of the researcher's caution is the widely held perception that people with disabilities are more vulnerable than almost anyone else, which then suggests that the researcher must proceed cautiously with the research task. This experience underscores the fact that the ethical base of research involving people with disabilities must proceed from the perspective of the research participants, not from the researcher's own understanding.[22]

The core of the ethical framework in doing research with a person with a disability centers around the relations between the researcher and that person. The idea of what constitutes friendship captures that core. When Shulamit Reinharz (1993) set herself the goal of studying friendships in a mental hospital, she discovered that her own understanding of what it means to have a friendship was solidly rooted in *her* world, not in the world of those living in the institution. She also discovered that a day-long friendship was the accepted norm in such an institution. In Reinharz's world, friendships extended over a long time, perhaps over a whole lifetime. Once she removed her own conceptions about friendship and began to understand the other meanings of friendship, she was able to obtain a clearer picture.

The researcher's understanding of the relationship between herself and the person with mental or emotional disabilities was key to the research performed by S. Anthony Thompson in a piece titled "My Researcher-friend? My Friend the Researcher? My Friend, My Researcher?: Conceptual and Procedural Issues of Informed Consent in Qualitative Research Methods for Persons with Developmental Disabilities" (2002). While generally the consent process is ongoing in most research settings, it becomes more difficult for the researcher to maintain the consent for research with people with mental disabilities because the relationship with the researcher is subject to constant change. The research participant moves the researcher into a position of varied roles: stranger, researcher, and friend. As Thompson notes,

> For persons with developmental disabilities, this confusion can become exacerbated. Researchers cannot assume that consent given *before* a project's commencement is the same as consent given *during* or *after* a project's completion. Simply stated, if research is ongoing, as is often the case using qualitative research strategies, so too is the informed-consent process. Individuals must be free to withdraw from participation at any time. Field researchers must take seriously the responsibility of *maintaining* participants' permission, since there are usually many consent difficulties that arise throughout a project's life span. (Thompson, 2002: 99)

The fact of having a disability, should not exclude the research participant from taking an active part in the research (Nind, 2011: 350).

Summary

Historically, qualitative researchers have had a long-standing interest in conducting research on, or with, people in vulnerable and marginal contexts. Many see the inductive nature of qualitative research as ideally suited to undertake this kind of research. Qualitative researchers have a nose for not pandering to prevailing views or solutions, making them suitable to research groups that have fallen beyond the ken of mainstream society, such as those who are homeless, elderly, incarcerated, or otherwise overlooked. If indeed the hallmark of society lies in the way it treats people in these contexts, then a qualitative researcher should feel no hesitation to study them. In a real sense, the qualitative researcher believes she can make a special contribution to understanding and analyzing people in these contexts, given her tools of the trade. What always stands out for a researcher is the vital need to be aware that powerless social groups require greater protection than the powerful, who, as Cloke et al. (2000: 135) remind us, "are able to protect themselves." The researcher often attempts to provide a "voice" to those who have been rendered voiceless or silent by society.

Chapter Ten

Organizational and Institutional Settings

Much of the research that has endured the test of time involves the study of organizations and institutions. One thinks of Howard Becker et al.'s *Boys in White* (1961), Rosabeth Moss Kanter's *Men and Women of the Corporation* (1977), and Eviatar Zerubavel's *Patterns of Time in Hospital Life* (1979). We have already touched upon the kinds of research participants who are likely to be the focus of our research, many of whom find themselves in organizational or institutional settings. Thus it is important to discuss in some detail the ethical dimensions of researching these larger settings—which include schools, prisons, nursing homes, the military, religious organizations, city councils, police departments, charities, ethics committees, hospitals, and the like. Each of these settings is different in its mission, social structure, components, functions, and hierarchy.

The Study of Organizations as a Potential Problem

The ethical dimensions surrounding the study of organizations[23] create a more complex picture than is the case for studying individuals and most other collectivities. From the moment a researcher embarks on a study of an organization, the integrity of the research will emerge as a sudden or potential problem. The argument that a group (a business, organization, governmental agency, or the like) should be studied "in the interest of

van den Hoonaard, Will C., and Deborah K. van den Hoonaard, "Organizational and Institutional Settings," in *Essentials of Thinking Ethically in Qualitative Research*, pp. 95–99. © 2013 Left Coast Press, Inc. All rights reserved.

public accountability" is not enough to convince the key decision-makers of such groups to permit research (Aldred, 2008: 893).

Even when an organization with the best of intentions invites a researcher to study it, the invitation may still sow the seeds of unavoidable problems because the integrity of the research (and researcher) is at stake. What if the researcher uncovers data that go against the party line of the organization? Would the suppression of data or analysis constitute a bona fide threat to academic freedom? What if the organization insists that the research not be published? The receipt of grants or monies heightens the potential to undermine research integrity because the grant-making organization often owns the data. Under these arrangements, the work can better be described as "contract research" than as "curiosity-driven research."

Permission to study an organization, as we know, does not always leave the ethics conundrum behind us. How does getting permission influence our research? The organization may well have given permission to study its official side, while the researcher's intentions may be closer to the academic side of research. In that connection, the researcher has to figure out how to get past the organization's party line if he is to present his findings with integrity. Similarly, when an organization's representative recommends whom the researcher should approach for interviews, etc., he may be likely to choose people who also represent the party line, thus allowing public image to assert itself in the research process.

Typically, researchers try to find people who have *not* been selected by the organization, in order to get a fuller picture. One of Will van den Hoonaard's colleagues always made a point of talking with the smokers in an organization, believing that much more can be gained from those who do not fit the mold as they congregate in clusters outside the back door of their company's building. What's more, smokers come from across the organization, share knowledge, and are more likely to have knowledge that crosses departments and the party line.

Ethical problems are exacerbated by public funders' recent proclivity for "partnerships" or "matching" funds from the private sector. These trends augur in an era where the topic or nature of research is no longer fully in the hands of the researcher.

Confidentiality

Interviewing individuals within an organization might create ethical dilemmas. Where loyalty to the organization is paramount, an employee may think that he is betraying the organization if he reveals to the researcher more than what is necessary. Of course, not all employees (or members of an organization) share the official point of view, in which case the researcher must take special care that confidentiality and anonymity be maintained. Especially in small organizations or settings that involve fewer people, a researcher should endeavor not to reveal where particular questions or issues come from.

All of us abide by particular expressions or idioms that make our speech immediately recognizable to those who know us. These distinctive expressions could betray the confidentiality bestowed on research participants because, in a closed setting, almost all would be familiar with one other. It would be impossible to maintain internal confidentiality. In organizational research, the researcher ought to make a greater than usual effort to foster confidentiality and anonymity so that no particular individual or organization can be blamed for structural failures that might detract from the issues being explored (see, e.g., Aldred, 2008: 895).

Highly structured organizations, such as urban hospitals and clinics, have a way of maintaining order and the status quo. A researcher's violating these hierarchical arrangements may bring difficulties for those with whom he has a working research relationship. It stands to reason that although anonymity and confidentiality are "portrayed in ethical frameworks as absolutes and universally positive" (Aldred, 2008: 895), people in hierarchical organizations are by no means on the same page on that score. Rachel Aldred found in her research on organizations that while some "demanded or expected confidentiality and anonymity, others wanted grievances and identities revealed" (2008: 895). Under those conditions, she advised, the researcher should give overwhelming weight to anonymity and confidentiality, even despite a participant's desire to bring grievances out into the open (Aldred, 2008: 895).

Faux Consent and Gatekeepers

Voluntary participation is a hallmark of ethical research, but in organizations there might be no room for truly "voluntary" participation. In these cases, we can speak of *faux consent*. For example, a military commander can order his men to participate in the research. Deborah Harrison faced this problem in her study of the military, *The First Casualty* (2002). From the perspective of social researchers, the nature of consent in the military is not meaningful if the order to participate in research comes from the commanding officer. From the soldier's perspective, it might not be so much about consent as about following orders—something that is on a higher scale of values than either giving consent or volunteering. One can imagine other settings where consent to participate in research is manufactured. For Piquemal (2001: 73), however, consent is only morally relevant if it comes from the person who has the authority to consent. Does this mean that a researcher need not ask soldiers for their consent because those in charge already have? The way out of such a dilemma would be not only to ask consent from the authority-in-charge but to also ask consent from the soldier. However, one of Deborah van den Hoonaard's graduate students told her that she thought the "volunteers" in her research could not get their heads around the idea of having a choice to participate.

Rachel Aldred points to similar problems in gaining consent in organizations in general. She "found the issue problematic when observing private meetings, being reliant upon gatekeepers to allow me access to the meeting, and to other participants, and to secure consent from the latter." She admitted that "[p]articularly where the gatekeeper was a senior manager, it was hard to know to what extent consent was really 'informed'" (Aldred, 2008: 895).

Another case of faux consent involves research of residents in a nursing home. The nursing home may want the researcher to get consent from the residents' families or other relatives, rather than from the resident, even when the resident is mentally competent. Similarly, studying a daycare center will inevitably involve securing consent from the children's parents.

Criminologists are more likely to encounter situations that involve organizations or institutions. Some study incarcerated populations while others are devoted to examining criminal-justice institutions that "perform a role as gatekeepers to researcher" (Israel, 2004: 18). In this connection, the "relatively powerful position of corporate and state bodies," Mark Israel suggests (2004: 18), "make[s] it particularly difficult to investigate their activities. Their work is complex, furtive, and ideologically masked."[24] No less troubling is the fact that criminologists are increasingly coopted by the state or corporations (Israel, 2004: 18).

It is not only criminologists who face the "problem" of gatekeepers. Nathalie Piquemal (2001: 68) raises this issue when a researcher encounters such gatekeepers as the band or tribal council on a reserve or reservation who defines what knowledge is legitimate. A researcher may come across a lot more than what the council defines as a "legitimate" topic of research.

Summary

Research on organizations and institutions begets a unique set of ethical dilemmas that are absent in other research. Securing permission seems a logical avenue to pursue, but the researcher must consider its implications in terms of what topics can or cannot be covered. Such permission may create a situation where only the official party line is voiced to the researcher. When a body confers a grant or contract on a researcher, additional ethical complications abound, leading the researcher into unspecified obligations. Such contract research flies in the face of curiosity-driven research. In highly structured organizations, such as the military, one can question the notion of consent, which, after all, is likely to be faux consent. Organizational gatekeepers intrude into the terrain of the research and can constitute a sincere problem for one's research.

Chapter Eleven

Qualitative Health Research

Qualitative health research embodies many of the kinds of research we've addressed so far, but there are essential differences in terms of its significant ethical dimensions. It is not easy to pin down a definition of health research. In some instances, faculty and students find themselves doing "health" research only because they are affiliated with an academic unit in the fields of health, such as nursing or kinesiology, while studying a topic that seems unrelated to physical or mental health. Most typically, qualitative health research is used to foster changes in practice and health policy (Macdonald and Carnevale, 2008). There is a nonapplied side, too, but it is less common. Politics, the weight of the biomedical paradigm of research, the condition and context of ill people, institutional gatekeeping, and the overriding emphasis on intervention point to particular ethical dimensions of qualitative health research. The impact of the hierarchy of credibility poses a particular ethical challenge to researchers. Qualitative health researchers will find themselves either in health-related organizations or in settings that involve only individuals outside of any organization.

Ill health stands outside the experience of many people, including researchers. Even physicians, says Janice Morse (2001: 317), "who may be considered experts in *disease* processes and who come into daily contact with the sick, may have had little personal experience with being ill." Thankfully, as Morse avers, qualitative researchers have risen to the challenge of understanding what it is like to be sick. Learning to step into the world of the ill lays a firm foundation for ethical research in this area.

Hierarchical Organizations

Health-care organizations tend to be more attuned to biomedical paradigms of research, to be hierarchical, and to involve gatekeepers. Qualitative research does not fit with conventional practices associated with research on health (and illness), such as clinical research, which uses different epistemological and ontological approaches (Macdonald and Carnevale, 2008: 2). This difference places qualitative health research in a political context. This context can define how qualitative research is understood and accepted in health circles, which in turn has implications for conducting research itself.

Many (nonqualitative) researchers believe that qualitative research runs against the idea of what "good" research is. Some will see qualitative health research as handmaidens to "real" research (Macdonald and Carnevale, 2008: 3), and that perception will affect the way opportunities may be shaped for qualitative researchers—which may affect the gathering of data. Nurses, doctors, health administrators, and midwives—all health professionals—have their own understanding of research. The qualitative researcher must invest some time and effort in educating health professionals about her approach.[25] At the same time, qualitative health researchers who seek to collaborate with health professionals, including physicians, will face "procedural ethics" where "informed consent . . . serves as a guiding moral light in research related to health" (Baarts, 2009: 432).

The power of hierarchy in medical settings came as a surprise to Lesley Conn. As a neophyte anthropologist, she was part of a multidisciplinary group researching the care for children born with various disorders of sexual development, and she wanted to learn how medicine influences people's ideas about gender (Conn, 2008: 501). She was very happy to learn that medical practitioners were pleased to have her on board, inviting her to operations and other backstage practices and consultations. After she introduced the doctors to her consent form, she was taken off-guard by their reluctance to sign the form. She surmised that doctors and clinicians were not used to having to subscribe to terms set out by others, namely "a graduate student, a non-doctor . . . and that these terms were non-negotiable" (Conn, 2008: 507). Although she eventually managed to develop a rapport with the research participants, feelings of great discomfort persisted. She writes that she is still "disheartened that the strenuous and generally unpleasant review process had some major consequences for me . . . in the field" (Conn, 2008: 508). The ensuing process to refine the consent form confirmed, in the eyes of the doctors and clinicians, that the research was not "ethical." The situation was resolved but not to everyone's satisfaction. Conn writes that "the request for a person's signature and the guarantee of anonymity is not only suspicious, but it sets the stage for a manufactured relationship, on terms set out beforehand" (Conn, 2008: 504). The consent form challenged the doctors' self-perception of being "in charge."

Ethical dilemmas arise from unsuspecting corners when doing research in health-related organizations, and those dilemmas largely come from what conventional researchers consider to be "real" science, namely biomedical research. When Christine Halse and Anne Honey (2005) conducted research among young women who believed they had anorexia, their ethics review committee forbade them from using self-diagnosis of anorexia. Instead, the researchers were forced to use medicalized terms. This instruction undid the actual purpose of the research by prohibiting the use of the expressions and thoughts of the young women themselves to explore what anorexia meant in their lives. Obtaining the perspective of research participants may not be a simple matter after all!

The ethical permutations of qualitative health research are complex. Professional hierarchies among medical practitioners, medical concepts of illness, inaccurate assessments regarding vulnerability, and the conflict of roles between being a carer and a researcher can misdirect a researcher from the original research plans. Another potential issue stems from the hierarchy of credibility—that is, when participants defer to people higher up in the organization, believing that they have more "expert" knowledge or are more believable.

Gatekeeping can also pose a problem, as Tina Miller discovered when trying to interview pregnant women in a Bangladeshi clinic (Miller and Bell, 2002: 61–63). A powerful gatekeeper could facilitate her access to those women. Because Miller was apprised that the women were "volunteered" for the research, she made sure that she provided a bona fide opportunity for them to "exercise some agency and to resist talking about certain aspects of their lives" (Miller and Bell, 2002: 62). Medical establishments, as mentioned earlier, are hierarchical, and the researcher must concentrate her efforts in getting consent at those supervisory levels while remaining faithful to the idea that she must provide room to research participants to give or withhold their own voluntary consent.

The Individual Research Participant

The bulk of the ethical dilemma resides in researching patients. Kate Holland (2007) voices a common worry about researching patients: are they well enough to give consent? She also warns that such fretful questions speak more of paternalism by the agencies that consent to this type of research than to something fundamentally inherent in patients (Holland, 2007: 905). The particular challenges that might evoke ethical dilemmas thus relate to special conditions of the sick person, who can be "silenced by disease," "muted by treatment," or "stunned by shock and pain" (Morse, 2001: 318–320).

Verina Wilde (1992: 237) points to the particular dilemma faced by nurse researchers (and perhaps other health researchers, too): while they "may be skilled at informal interviewing and counseling in their clinical role," they need to remind themselves that their aim in collecting data is for research, not for the purposes of intervention or providing therapy.

The close relationship between the researcher and the patient/research participant brings the question of power to the fore. Where does power reside in that relationship? When a patient is seriously ill, a conscientious researcher will tend to accord more power to the patient, out of feelings of respect and sympathy, but there are also (im)balances of power that are not evident. What stands out is the perceived or actual vulnerability of the patient, and the researcher cannot take anything for granted as far as that is concerned. This heightened sense of vulnerability leads a researcher to give more thought to the need for protection, dignity, and privacy. Finally, when a researcher's academic "home" is a medical one, particular ethical issues arise when she is both a caregiver and a researcher at the same time. This relationship alters conventional relationships with a research participant. The researcher is no longer the interested listener whose presence is measured only in hours. But when the research participant relies on the researcher for care and/or therapy, the notion of voluntary participation becomes a source of potential conflict (Holloway and Wheeler, 1995).

The researcher, however, should not be overly swayed by arguments that patients are too fragile or vulnerable (Holland, 2007) and that in-depth interviews will necessarily lead to great harm. There is no evidence (as shown in Chapter Five) to suggest that interviews result in any greater harm than everyday life (Corbin and Morse, 2003).

Anonymity in health research may be difficult to achieve. Some ill people have noticeably intrusive symptoms that would make them quite easily identifiable by friends, family, and colleagues. We already cited the example of Joyce Kennedy's research (2005) in a school for children with hearing problems.

Summary

Whether conducting research in health-related organizations (such as hospitals and nursing homes) or researching individuals outside of organizational settings, the researcher will encounter special ethical challenges. In health-care settings, the hierarchy of structure and of expertise pose unique challenges, as does gatekeeping. When researching individuals affected by poor health or illness, researchers must be mindful of the potential power imbalance. However, the researcher should not underestimate the ability of research participants to consent (or not) to the research. The researcher should also be mindful of the tendency of such research toward therapy rather than research proper.

Chapter Twelve

Writing, Publishing, and Representation

For many, one of the most painful stages in research is writing up the data. A student who is writing a PhD dissertation has already struggled with the most significant questions about writing: is this what my research participants want me to write about them? How much should I, as researcher, insert myself as a person in the dissertation? Are my findings authentic? For whom am I writing? These are good questions to raise because they do not disappear after completing the dissertation, and they are supremely ethical in nature. These questions revolve around three ingredients of ethical writing: the research participants, the author/writer/researcher, and the reader.[26]

The Research Participants

Every author experiences anxiety when publishing his first article or book. One source of anxiety goes straight to the origins of his research, namely the research participants. Will those whom he interviewed and also allowed him to write up *their* data be disappointed with his publication? Will the publication reveal the true purpose of his research? Will his publication still afford them anonymity (if that is their wish)? These gut feelings are genuine. Even veteran authors continue to live with those inescapable thoughts. There is something to be said about

van den Hoonaard, Will C., and Deborah K. van den Hoonaard, "Writing, Publishing, and Representation," in *Essentials of Thinking Ethically in Qualitative Research*, pp. 107–113. © 2013 Left Coast Press, Inc. All rights reserved.

exploring these thoughts, which can help move the publication of the work in an ethical direction.

Researchers generally feel no end of gratitude to those who have given so much of their time and support to their work. That gratitude manifests itself in various ways: first, through formal acknowledgments of their contributions; and second, through the manner in which he treats their data, avoiding at all costs the destruction of data. Research participants can feel unsettled by the ready manner of destroying their data. A fair, balanced, nonjudgmental stance while writing up the data and performing their analysis suggests that a researcher has done his homework.

There are a number of inherent challenges with social research. Many researchers aver that if one's research does not upset someone, the research is not up to standard. Consider that a social researcher is in the business of critically analyzing social settings. A researcher cannot be satisfied with the status quo. The researcher has a responsibility to pay attention to issues of social justice and equality. If the researcher faithfully mirrors the studied society or group, he is making a contribution to the life of society. The researcher should hold on to the idea that because he has researched many people, he will know more about the setting than any single research participant (Becker, 1998: 99).

The ethical strain in publishing one's research is to balance an acknowledgment of the research participants' contributions without taking away from the essential purpose of the research, which is analysis. There are a number of strategies that help achieve this balance. Will van den Hoonaard tried to achieve such a balance in his study of a religious community (1996). After completing an early draft, he shared it with a cross section of community members, women and men, older and relatively younger. He then convened the whole group to a roundtable at a Chinese restaurant where each could share his or her insights about the manuscript. What emerged was a more meaningful (but nonpandering) book. He also acknowledged them specifically in the book.

Another way to verify the gathered information is to engage in "member checking," also known as informant feedback, external validity, or fittingness (Morse et al., 2002). Some researchers see member checking as an extension of informed consent (Crow et al., 2006: 92). Usually, member checking occurs immediately after the interview, although one could also say that sharing the findings or analyses with research participants is a form of member checking. When member checking involves group therapy, Melissa Harper and Patricia Cole (2012: 510) believe that it is "an important quality control process in qualitative research" by which a researcher "seeks to improve the accuracy, credibility and validity" of the recording.

The researcher returns the transcript to the interview participant and asks him to make "corrections." There can be problems with this approach, both of a practical and a theoretical nature. First, the interview participant has already been generous with his time with the interview, and to ask him to "correct" the transcript may be an undue burden. Second, as the transcript contains normal speech and language patterns, the participant may be distracted and tempted to correct them (Crow et al., 2006: 92). There is also the urge to rephrase ideas, sometimes to make them conform to the party line even though the intention of the interview might be not about that. Harper and Cole (2012: 514) also remind researchers that member checking may trigger "overwhelming feelings" and "negative emotions" when participants read their own personal statements. Third, according to Wiles et al. (2006: 294), member checking has implications for the "freedom of the researcher to interpret the data in the way she or he views as appropriate." The question then remains: how can a researcher "balance the rights or needs of the participant with the needs of the research and the researcher" (Wiles et al., 2006: 294)? One could argue, too, that finding such a balance is neither possible nor desirable.

Referring to the work of Linda Caissie (2006), we learn that member checking had a negative effect on her research about the Raging Grannies, a women's activist group. Not only did her interview participants begin to reshape their personal perspectives into "official" statements about the Raging Grannies after the transcripts were returned to them, but a number withdrew their participation from the research because of the extra work it involved, although only a few were embarrassed by seeing how the transcript conveyed their everyday speech. Caissie had interviewed twenty-eight women, but in the end, only fifteen bothered to go over their own interview transcripts (personal communication from L. Caissie, 4 July 2012).

Finally, member checking inadvertently misrepresents the research to the interview participant. Research is about a whole slew of interviews, and the researcher is seeking patterns involving the culling of selected materials from interviews. This last point speaks to the problem of (re) presentation and "voice" in research. When a researcher relies on a large slew of interviews (and selects only narrow segments), can one still speak about actual "representation of voice"? Moreover, the lengthy and cumbersome process of member checking might lead the participant to believe that his voice will be individually represented.

The Researcher

The current pace of research in the social sciences is producing side effects that were unthinkable years ago. While adapting to these new circumstances, one finds new ethical exigencies, specifically those of multiple authorship and what one researcher has dubbed "salami" publishing (Blancett, 1991).

Multiple authorship can pose a grave risk to the integrity of research. Because this is a relatively new phenomenon, we must look for insights from other disciplines although they may not easily fit the social-science framework. Both biomedical and natural-sciences research have struggled valiantly to cast the issue of multiple authorship into a workable ethical framework. The pressures of publishing and securing research grants are spilling out of the ethical framework, however.

As can be expected, the ethics of multiple authorship takes place on a continuum. At one extreme, as is current among the natural sciences, a publication carries the names of anyone who is attached to the research (usually a lab)—from the supervisor who secured the grant, to those who analyzed the results, to the actual writers of the publication, and all those who worked in the laboratory even if they did not work on the particular piece of published research. At the other end, a publication may include as few names as possible (such as in some of the social sciences and the humanities, in particular). Some believe that in participatory-action research, the authorship should include the name of the community or the names of anyone who participated in the research. Careful attention needs then to be paid to not losing the anonymity of research participants, especially when the name of the community appears as author. These are disciplinary habits that add a dimension of conflicting scientific cultures. Articles with the longest list of authors fall in the natural sciences and medicine,[27] with the social sciences having much shorter lists of authors.

Given the vast array of practices within and among disciplines (and between cultures), it is difficult to establish an ethical norm to govern all disciplines.[28] On the whole, though, there is agreement that listed authors should have substantially contributed to the research. However, there are differences of opinion as to what constitutes a "substantial" contribution. To the research alone? To the writing? To providing the research grant that made the research possible? Should names be listed in alphabetical order? Should "honorary authors" (such as heads of departments) be listed? There is now widespread agreement that "ghost authorship" is ethically objectionable, but it was (and still is) something that the pharmaceutical industry engaged in: an insider in the company writes up the article but invites a well-known researcher to append his name as "author." One can see how the inner ethical poise needs to come to the fore because conventions in disciplines seem to fly in the face of ethics and the pressure to follow these conventions is hard to ignore or discount.

The question of "salami" publications (Blancett, 1991) raises a different specter. The term refers to the trend of slicing up one's research into smaller and smaller publishable papers. The eagerness to see one's work appear multiple times, each time from a different angle, speaks to the urgency of wanting to establish oneself as a scholar who can contribute to the field. The main risk attached to salami publications is the danger of citing oneself repeatedly. *The Journal of Academic Ethics* (Bretag and Mahmud, 2009) speaks of "self-plagiarism" when authors are impelled to cite the same words (and ideas) without sourcing themselves.

The Reader

For the most part, it is relatively easy to visualize the readers, or audience, of one's publication. A dissertation begets the PhD committee and a few external readers. A dissertation published as a book takes in a much wider circle of readers. Both content and style can express an ethical approach. Generally, the ethical principles that guide the work of researchers vis-à-vis research participants also guide how we ought to approach our readers. The primary ethical key is dignity. More precisely, it is about preserving the dignity of the reader.

In a climate of divisive politics, protests, and demonstrations, it might be hard to conceive of any approach that does not involve these aspects of society. We breathe them in through the air around us. Scholarship can be persuasive. However, to achieve such an enviable goal, it is best for a scholar to respect the dignity of the reader. But what does that involve?

The author must leave the reader some room to make up his own mind. No matter the research topic, there is always a side to be taken or sympathized with. Topics may range from labor disputes, to seal hunting, to euthanasia, to abortion, and so on. The range of emotionally laden topics is endless, and there is no lack of taking sides in these matters. Scholarship presents as many sides as possible in a manner that does not take away the reader's decision to take one side or another. Yes, the author can let the reader know on what side he falls, but what actually matters is how the side that is *not* favored by the author is treated. The reader may already be on the author's side or may not have yet made up his mind. But the author should not force the reader to make a decision by virtue of lambasting one of the sides. That decision should be left to the reader. This approach requires finesse, but it can be learned. Fortunately, there are so many sides on any issue that a researcher can easily exercise his skills in presenting his case with an open mind.

Almost inevitably, as a researcher gains experience in conducting research and writing up data, the notion of being an "expert" enters into the realm of writing. Is there room for making recommendations after one's analysis or for suggesting what should be considered "best practice"? Given the vast variety of research themes, topics, and strategies, it is impossible to provide a definitive, all-encompassing answer to these questions. If anything, the goal of the researcher is to preserve and promote the dignity of the reader. It will become apparent whether or not ending one's research with a set of recommendations will support the notion of the reader's dignity. Of particular note is *knowledge translation*—a term that is now in vogue to refer to the process of "translating" one's research findings to practical settings. Chapter 14 provides a full discussion of this term.

Summary

Publishing one's research represents the final step in a research undertaking. The three main parties implicated in publishing are the research participants, the researcher, and the reader. No single ethical approach can satisfy all angles. In terms of the research participants, the researcher must be frank about his findings. Without pandering to the claims of research participants, the researcher needs to be analytical. Member checking seems to be a justifiable part of any research, but there are important shortcomings that may vex the researcher. And if the issue of "voice" and "representation" are important, should the researcher accede to the research participant's wish not to be anonymized? The social-scientific approach can go a long way in addressing some of this ethical strain.

Chapter Thirteen

Research-Ethics Review

Increasingly, social research is being streamed through university ethics committees, known as institutional review boards (IRBs) in the United States, research ethics boards (REBs) in Canada, local ethics committees (LECs) in the United Kingdom, and so on. We have deliberately saved our discussion of these boards and committees for the last section of the book.

For many students, "going through ethics" has become a new benchmark in progressing through a graduate program. While students can typically prepare themselves to defend a thesis proposal (or mount an oral defense of the thesis) with the help of fellow students and a supervisor, it can be challenging to know what an ethics committee is looking for. To be sure, there are checklists, prepared online forms, and insights shared by members of one's peer group who have gone before.

Although usually not insurmountable, the challenges become more critical when there has been a change in ethics-committee membership or chair, when particular ethical issues wax or wane each year, and/or when the researcher's topic or method of research deviates from the norm. As if the challenge were not difficult enough, the researcher must take into account the nature of historical relations between the ethics committee and researchers, in addition to her supervisor's personal attitude towards research-ethics review, which sometimes makes the student

van den Hoonaard, Will C., and Deborah K. van den Hoonaard, "Research Ethics Review," in *Essentials of Thinking Ethically in Qualitative Research*, pp. 115–121. © 2013 Left Coast Press, Inc. All rights reserved.

rely more heavily on what the chair of the ethics committee advises as the "appropriate" strategy of research. It's understandable that some confuse the terms *ethical review* and *ethics review*. It is more correct to use the less-charged term *ethics review*. Whether the review proceeded along "ethical" lines is sometimes a matter of debate.

The researcher can face multiple challenges when addressing ethical issues. First, it is difficult to pin down precisely what ethics committees are looking for. In each country, although one research-ethic code guides the work of these boards and committees, there are considerable variations. These variations can be so great that one would be hard-pressed to write a handbook on how to "get through ethics" that would be useful across all universities,

Second, because we are painfully aware that the source and nature of research-ethics guidelines initially trace back to the needs of biomedical research, the offered paradigm of ethics does not always speak to the ethical needs of social researchers, let alone qualitative researchers. The "one mold for all" is something that social researchers have been struggling with for the past two or three decades. A growing number of book-length publications wrestle with the biomedical basis of research-ethics codes for the social sciences, such as those by Zachary Schrag (2010), Will van den Hoonaard (2011), and Laura Stark (2011), as have numerous articles.[29] Some books, like *Ethical Futures in Qualitative Research: Decolonizing the Politics of Knowledge* (Denzin and Giradina, 2007), have set themselves the goal of finding and creating space in ethics-review systems while advancing the tenets of qualitative research.

Third, we are striving for more universal conceptions of qualitative research. There is a patchwork of decisions among ethics committees that seem contradictory to each other. Some ethics committees give carte blanche to oral historians to conduct oral research while others subject oral-history proposals to a full review (Shopes, 2002; W. van den Hoonaard, 2011: 180). Some committees insist that the researcher use consent forms, while for others an information letter is adequate. Some research applications for ethics review commit the researcher not to deviate from the guidelines for questions in interviews. Others do not. In some universities, some kinds of research are classified as "quality assurance" and are therefore exempt from ethics review, while others make no such exemption. The list is endless.

Fourth, it would be too complex an issue to help one work through the many levels of research-ethics review ("vertical ethics"), given that academic departments, grant committees, scholarly journals, and schools of graduate studies are seized by varying standards of ethical research. This structure of "vertical ethics" is sometimes quite bewildering (W. van den Hoonaard, 2011: 277–82). It will never be appropriate or possible for a textbook to offer detailed advice in that area.

Fifth, a textbook such as ours cannot predict the fads in research-ethics review. Such notions as third-party liability, member checking, the destruction of data or archiving all data, protecting researchers when abroad, the use of signed consent forms, or confidentiality in focus groups appear unheralded, stay for awhile, and then sometimes disappear. Some ethics fads stick around longer than others.

The soundest approach asks the researcher to be aware of the universal and contextual ethical principles of doing qualitative research—the real foundation of thinking ethically—and then figure out the approach that is taken in her university to "get through ethics." The matching up of universal principles of doing qualitative research, on one hand, with the research-ethics review process, on the other, is not always successful, but it is the system currently in place. Carolyn Ells (2011), among others, offers sobering insights as to what qualitative researchers can expect from ethics committees. Her article is a useful tool in recognizing the "needs" of ethics committees and what they hope to see in qualitative-research applications.

Preparing Your Case for the Research Ethics Board

The process of submitting an application to an ethics committee can be intimidating. Terms like *investigator, protocol, best practice, evidence-based research*, and *research study design* have seeped into common ethics terminology, whereas qualitative researchers would more typically use terms like *researcher, research plan*, or *interview guide*. The term *best practice* suggests there is only one approach, whereas qualitative researchers claim many practices, depending on the setting, topic, and research participants. In this context, the idea of a best practice is a fallacy. As field researchers Jack Haas and William Shaffir (2009: 1113) indicate, fieldworkers and researchers know "there is no single best 'cookbook' for conducting field research, or," citing Vidich et al. (1964: vii), "disentangling the practice of their method from social influence." The term

"How did you ever get this past an ethics board?"

This is the first question I face after delivering my job talk. The previous forty minutes have been spent outlining my ethnographic research into a subculture of male "pickup artists," a community of men who trade strategies on how to attract and seduce women. The hiring committee facing me has been tasked with filling a tenure-track position focused on qualitative methodology.

The ethical concern being expressed is over my ambivalence toward the men's behavior. How could I observe and even assist them as they used canned routines and strategies in the pursuit of sex? Why did I not intervene? Was I not obligated to stop bad people from doing bad things? I am far from the first ethnographer to observe or aid deviant behavior. But there is a politics to the ethics of studying deviant groups. Where does the group fit in the hierarchy of power and credibility? In my case, they (men) are "top dogs" and their perceived victims (women) are not. Had I chosen to study graffiti artists or the passive resistance of student antiwar protestors, would the question of my obligations to stop the activities being observed loom as large?

Those who study the sociology of deviance often practice a forced ambivalence toward the morality of their subjects' behavior. But this ambivalence is not shared across the discipline, and it is imperative that young scholars be aware of this. Ethics review does not end with one's institutional review board. Hiring committees, journal editors, and anonymous manuscript reviewers will all evaluate the ethics of our research. Their perception is key and their ambivalence not guaranteed. Those embarking on the research that will shape their early careers must carefully consider how the politics of ethics review will impact the reception given to their research, not only by ethics boards, but also by the gatekeepers of their academic careers. –Anthony Christensen, Wilfrid Laurier University at Brantford, Ontario, Canada *evidence-based research* provokes wonder because qualitative researchers have long spoken about using data as evidence and as a starting point for research, rather than trying to fit data into a theoretical construct.

Ethics committees have become increasingly insistent that researchers provide research participants with a consent form. Qualitative researchers, as a rule, have resisted using such a form. Crow et al. (2006: 88–91) adhere to the idea that the form tends to make it more difficult to research people in vulnerable settings, ethnic groups, and the aged. Some groups will never get studied, such as those whose members have dementia. Crow et al. also point out that pulling out a consent form for a signature makes it harder to develop rapport with the participant and, as a consequence, harder to get authentic data. Research participants, moreover, see the form as a bureaucratic procedure, which can antagonize people. Finally, the use of the form faces practical problems, such as when researching sick people.

However, Crow et al. (2006: 83–87) also believe that there are some benefits when ethics committees advocate the use of consent forms. In preparing such forms, the researcher has more lead time to think through the issue of what constitutes consent, leading him to reflect about getting relevant information from research participants. Ethics committees believe that a good consent process leads to trust and rapport, resulting in obtaining better data. They also aver that a good form results in a higher participation rate because the research participant has received convincing assurances. Aside from having divergent perspectives about what constitutes consent, the idea of protecting research participants from harm also induces a diversity of opinion between ethics committees and researchers about what is a harm or a benefit (Mayan, 2009: 126, 127). Following Morse et al. (2008), there are at least six ways of understanding risk or harm: (1) experiences or characteristics that would make the research participant vulnerable (such as trauma); (2) topics that make the research participant feel vulnerable (death of a loved one); (3) relationship with the researcher (such as becoming too involved); (4) the setting ("environment" such as the home); (5) potential outcome of the research; or (6) whether the researcher finds it hard to handle a topic or finds herself in danger.

The most satisfying approach would be to discuss the nature of one's research with a member of the university ethics committee, preferably its chair, to tease out the relevant ethical dilemmas that attend to qualitative research and to a specific study. If a student is doing the research, it is advisable to secure ideas from the supervisor. A faculty member might find it useful to discuss the process with a colleague.

If the application does not turn out to be routine, one hopes that one's department can render assistance, either by showing the best avenue of handling the situation or by standing fully behind the student when the ethics committee raises objections or major questions. Teachers should not leave a student alone to handle these issues.

More than once, researchers have noted that an "individual-focused, biomedically oriented approach to IRB review" of projects that involve participatory-action research (Malone et al., 2006: 1,915) has privileged the protection of institutional power structures and the perpetuation of inequality rather than creating social change in the community.

What stands the researcher in good stead is intimately knowing the paragraphs, sections, or chapters of research-ethics policies that deal specifically with qualitative research or that the ethics committee uses to deal with qualitative research. In the United States, there are no specific sections that can be relied on to provide guidance on doing ethical qualitative research. Even a few years ago, the United States Department of Health and Human Services (Secretary, 2009) still identified the following areas as among the many challenges university-based IRBs face as they review applications for community-based participatory research: risks and harms for groups and small communities; determining when "research" actually begins and what constitutes a modification that must be reviewed (changes are often iterative as researchers interact with the community); understanding the role of community member-researchers; the process of collaborating with communities to develop research strategies and the likely need to accommodate in-course corrections and changes; and *qualitative research methods.*

In Canada, chapter 10 of the *Tri-Council Policy Statement on Ethical Research Involving Humans* (CIHR et al., 2010) offers up-to-date help in guiding researchers to do ethical qualitative research.

In the United Kingdom, the *Framework for Research Ethics* of the Economic and Social Council displays an in-depth understanding of qualitative research methods in light of how risks might be understood and the developing nature of research. The *Framework* even offers a case study on how ethics committee can evaluate a qualitative research project (ESRC, 2010).

In Australia, chapter 3.1 of the *National Statement on Ethical Conduct in Human Research* (NHMRC, 2007) succinctly covers various aspects of ethics in qualitative research, including life story or oral history, focus groups, observation, archival research, online research, and action research.

Summary

Over the course of any research project, ethical dilemmas may unexpectedly emerge. While there are some very broad ethical principles at work, virtually all other principles rely on ethical reflection on a case-by-case basis. It is good to invoke the experiences of supervisors, colleagues, and ethics committees. One should become familiar with how other researchers have handled ethical dilemmas, as well as with the relevant sections of applicable national ethics codes that touch on qualitative research.

Chapter Fourteen

Ethics Lag

This brief chapter discusses the "ethics lag" whereby ethics policies are outstripped by the routines and exigencies of everyday life that influence the research-ethics review process, on one hand, and developments in qualitative methods, on the other.

The Contemporary Routines of Everyday Life

Unlike in the past, scholarly disciplines have become intermeshed with everyday life, and boundaries are now more permeable. Many everyday phenomena and interests are now bleeding into research. One example comes from the culture's increasing reliance on individualism and the importance of personal space, so often expressed in self-help movements and ideas about self-esteem.

Much of contemporary qualitative research is emerging from our culture's insistence on personal space, including that of the researcher. For example, Andrea Doucet's research for her book, *Do Men Mother?* (2006), was inspired by her childhood curiosity about why her neighbors had misgivings about a single father across the street who was raising four children. While past researchers worked with personal space, its relevance was seldom acknowledged or discussed, let alone celebrated. Recasting research in terms of personal space is something that ethics guidelines do not address. The question then is how do those guidelines fit into the "new" research? Should they? Is it possible to fit such concerns into an ethical straitjacket? Do we need to reshape guidelines so that there is a more obvious connection between personal space in one's research and ethics? What would such a connection look like?

We can attribute the rise of narratives and autoethnographies as scholarly styles to society's interest in storytelling. The blurring of boundaries between everyday life and research can create unsettling feelings about whether principles from standard research-ethics codes can really apply to "research" whose origins lie in popular culture. From the perspective of researchers, attempts to apply a system of ethics originally designed from the perspective of biomedical research seem contrived and ill suited to the task. We know that the ethical dimensions involving research from a personal space differ from research starting from an "objective" place.

The realms of law and ethics, however, remain one of the most urgent matters for all researchers and ethics committees because they deeply shape research in terms of academic freedom, responsibility, and integrity. These matters deal with legal liability, consent, privacy, and confidentiality. It is easy to see how notions of law and legal liability drift into ethical areas. In the United States, the Common Rule for the Protection of Human Subjects for Behavioral and Social Science Research stipulates that the "major goal is to limit harms to participants in research" (NSF, 2002). The U.S. Code of Federal Regulations (United States Department of Health and Human Services, 2009: §46.101, §46.408) sidesteps potential conflicts between ethics and law and seems to advocate the subservience of ethics to law.

In Canada's original policies on ethics and research, ethics and law stood as separate issues, but the revised policies (*TCPS 2*) clearly shifted toward making ethics conform to law (CIHR et al., 2010: Chapter 1):

> Researchers may face situations where they experience a tension between the requirements of the law and the guidance of the ethical principles in this Policy. In such situations, researchers should strive to comply with the law in the application of ethical principles. Researchers should consult with colleagues, the REB or any relevant professional body, and if necessary, seek independent legal advice to help resolve any conflicts between law and ethics, and guide an appropriate course of action.

A more stringent application of laws resides in the United Kingdom's *Framework for Research Ethics* (ESRC, 2010: 1.17.2.4, 1.17.4.3), under which data can only be obtained through lawful purposes and which places limits on confidentiality. Australia's statement on ethics in research (NHMRC, 2007: 8, 9, 67, 74) not only makes ethical conduct in research subservient to law but also mandates that at least one lawyer be part of university ethics committees (81). Indeed, much social research could be curtailed when one merely considers legal liability for the university.

The End of Privacy?

Despite all the measures put in place by national ethics codes and legislation affirming the importance of privacy, one could argue that we are entering an era that is witnessing the end to privacy. Ubiquitous use of technology and the rise of the surveillance society are eliminating privacy by localizing and personalizing global knowledge of family, friends, acquaintances, and strangers, much like the practice of villages and small towns of times past.

One of the major intrusions of everyday life into the world of research-ethics review relates to technology and the very vast world of the Internet in particular. Technology produces an ethics lag with far-ranging conundrums dealing with issues of privacy, intellectual property rights, trust, and authenticity (Convery and Cox, 2012: 51). The ethical cornerstone is privacy and confidentiality. Texts and images have become so ubiquitous that it would be unreasonable for researchers to treat them any differently than common usage dictated by popular practice. A number of court rulings on Twitter, for example, indicate that Twitter messages cannot be considered private: they are in the public domain. Does the researcher still need consent to use Twitter postings? YouTube images are now so commonplace that even the most private, violent, or morally degrading acts (involving citizens, law-enforcement agencies, and other institutions) get air time, sometimes viewed by millions of people around the globe.

The rise of the surveillance society as a result of technological developments casts research ethics in a new light. There is an ironic balance between the relentless exposure of ordinary citizens to videocams, face-recognition software, and the like while researchers must find a way to secure ethics approval to bring these aspects into their research. Will researchers, under these conditions, affirm their approval of the surveillance society, or should researchers stay away as far as possible from the current trend of more surveillance?

Finally, the relentless drift toward the idea of accountability has already flowed into research-ethics review. Indeed, the thrust of ethics committees in universities (and elsewhere) is to see themselves as promoting accountability for research undertaken under their aegis. When researchers hear of "higher" ethics standards for evaluating research, should they be comforted, or should they worry that "higher" standards will produce more bureaucratic paperwork without necessarily improving any ethical standards?

New Thrusts in the Application of Research

It is impossible to predict which new features of qualitative research will replace or coexist with current paradigms. However, one major thrust is already looming on the horizon—namely the drive for applied research and research that involves knowledge translation (KT) or translational research. Previously reserved for think tanks, private agencies, and corporations (including hospitals), the ideals of knowledge translation are seeping into scholarly granting bodies. Knowledge translation refers to making research "applied." No doubt, this trend is closely allied with the accountability society (referred to above) to make researchers more accountable, not necessarily on wider scholarly terms but in terms of narrow relevance to society. One of Canada's research-granting agencies (Canadian Institutes for Health Research) provides the following description of knowledge translation:

> a dynamic and iterative process that includes synthesis, dissemination, exchange and ethically-sound application of knowledge to improve the health of Canadians, provide more effective health services and products and strengthen the health care system. . . . This process takes place within a complex system of interactions between researchers and knowledge users which may vary in intensity, complexity and level of engagement depending on the nature of the research and the findings as well as the needs of the particular knowledge user. (CIHR, 2012)

Not much is known about the overarching ethical dilemmas that knowledge translation can create. Because one visualizes knowledge translation as a one-way street—from the researcher to the "knowledge user"—there is no room for the transfer of knowledge from the patient to the researcher (see D. van den Hoonaard, 2009). Interestingly, in such a conceptual scheme ("from the bench to the bedside") the clinicians, not the patients, are the "users." A qualitative researcher looks askance at the one-way model of knowledge translation given the inductive nature and dynamic process of research. Advocates of knowledge translation have ignored the profound ethical implications when researchers cast research participants as "users" rather than as active agents who may also have something valuable to contribute.

What role do professional or academic associations play in formulating the proper, ethical course of action for their researchers? For example, an association might not agree as to what might constitute "harm" in research. Such is the case of the Human Terrain System program of the United States military in Iraq and Afghanistan, when the American Anthropological Association had to wrestle with the moral dilemma of anthropologists' conducting research on behalf of the military. Some anthropologists claimed that their research on the populations would foster "less harm" than when the military was unfamiliar with the local cultures. As Scott Jaschik asks, is this "a moral standard worthy of consideration or a cop out?" He further asks, "Should scholars talk about their conduct during wartime in a general way without regard to the war taking place? . . . Should scholars take a firm stand against any involvement?" (Jaschik, 2007: 1).

Commercialism in universities provides another ethics lag that produces serious ethical quandaries with unforeseen consequences. Mintz et al. (2010) identified a number of conflicts that have invaded university teaching and research. When universities secure corporate grants to mount courses and research, curricula and other issues "may be slanted to promote the interests of a corporation or other provider of outside funding" (Mintz et al., 2010: 1). To take a specific, obvious example, would students (and faculty) be reluctant to research the antiunion or antilabor practices of a corporation that has generously donated to the university? In more general terms, would social research become more quietist and less critical of the status quo? Governments and others have so aggressively pursued corporate support for universities that the inner ethical poise of researchers may become a quaint relic of the past, practiced by those who already have tenure.

The contemporary rush to secure research grants for personal and professional advancement obscures significant ethical problems. As Rachel Aldred (2008: 894) avers, "[c]ontract research, and the need to keep and win contracts, creates pressures on researchers and makes it important that they are provided with the advice and support necessary to gain acceptable rights over data, methods, etc., from sponsors and funders." No less relevant is the strong possibility that "mission-driven" research can undermine the ethical premises of one's research. This can take a variety of forms, from a research sponsor's specifying what ought (or ought not) to be researched, to establishing the problem purely from an agency's perspective. What is one to make of research funded by a social-work agency about the plight of the homeless? What kinds of spin in the research do nursing-home administrators place on research in "their" nursing home? These are profound ethical perturbations that are not always touched upon by ethics codes, especially in this climate of "rush research."[30] The ramping up of the speed of research undercuts reflexivity and endangers the researcher's inner moral poise.

Summary

This chapter has touched upon the ethics lag as it pertains to qualitative research. Individualism (with its emphasis on highlighting personal space) and the popular love for storytelling have both invaded research space. These intrusions raise questions about the appropriateness of formal ethics codes that are (still) based on a biomedical paradigm. Considerable ethics lag exists in the realm of law and ethics as researchers and policy makers try to decide which comes first in research: ethics or law?

Much of the ethics lag is due to the phenomenal development and growth of technology and the rise of the surveillance society. Technology is breaking down the barriers to privacy and confidentiality (which are the hallmark of ethics in research). Do we as researchers pander to these shifting moral perspectives, or do we resist these trends?

Similarly, should researchers adapt society's drive to accountability at face value or do we see that the emperor has no clothes? If ethics committees thrive on the idea of accountability, should we take the increased paperwork for granted?

Ethical issues loom even larger when one considers two significant cultural trends: on one hand, the promotion of knowledge transfer/translation, which runs counter to the whole idea of qualitative research with its advocacy of inductive research, and, on the other hand, the pressures to speed up publishing the research, which can undercut reflexivity and endangers the researcher's inner moral poise.

Online Resources

Australia and New Zealand

Australian Sociological Association
www.tasa.org.au/about-tasa/ethical-guidelines
Describes the organization's code of ethics, which draws on internationally accepted principles.

Sociological Association of Aotearoa New Zealand
https://sites.google.com/site/nzsociology/Resources
Provides guidelines for ethical behavior and decision making with respect to research, teaching, publishing, and professional conduct.

Canada

Panel on Research Ethics
www.pre.ethics.gc.ca
Starting point for Tri-Council Policy Statement: Ethical Conduct for Research Involving Humans. Chapter 10 of TCPS provides additional information on qualitative-research ethics. See: www.pre.ethics.gc.ca/eng/ policy-politique/initiatives/tcps2-eptc2/chapter10-chapitre10/

Research Ethics in the Social Sciences and Humanities
www.researchethics.ca/social-science-humanities.htm
Provides an overview of research ethics in the social sciences and humanities, including geography, history, political science, anthropology, economics, psychology, criminology, and sociology along with literature, philosophy, theology, visual and performing arts, and cultural studies.

Canadian Sociological Association
www.csa-scs.ca/code-of-ethics
The CSA updated its own code of ethics after the release of TCPS 2 (see above), specifically addressing concerns about "ethics creep."

United Kingdom

Oral History Society
www.ohs.org.uk/ethics/index.php
Provides a primer on ethics for researchers who record oral-history interviews and organizations and individuals who keep collections of oral-history recording.

British Criminology Department
www.britsoccrim.org/codeofethics.htm
The code of ethics for researchers in the field of criminology promotes the highest ethical standards in criminological research.

British Sociological Association
www.britsoc.co.uk/equality/#_cancant
Contains ethical practice guidelines that speak at length to what sociologists can and cannot do as an association.

Social Research Association
http://the-sra.org.uk/wp-content/uploads/ethics03.pdf
The SRA's downloadable Ethics Guidelines are applicable to "all who practice, use or have an interest in social research."

British Educational Research Association
http://bera.dialsolutions.net/system/files/3/BERA-Ethical-Guidelines-2011.pdf/

Offers bibliographies on ethics regulations, discusses conflict among principles, deals with situated judgments and the basis of informed consent and related contracts.

United States

American Anthropological Association
http://aaanet.org/issues/policy-advocacy/Protecting-Human-Subjects.cfm
The AAA's policy on protecting human subjects outlines anthropologists' moral obligations as members of groups, as well as scholars.

American Sociological Association
www.asanet.org/about/ethics.cfm
Sets forth the principles and ethical standards that underlie sociologists' professional responsibilities and conduct.

Qualitative Research Consultants Association
www.qrca.org/displaycommon.cfm?an=1&subarticlenbr=21
The QRCA's code of ethics reflects the organization's belief that its members must uphold the highest standards of ethical and professional behavior, not only in their work, but in their relationships with clients, field suppliers, colleagues, and respondents.

International

International Sociological Association
www.isa-sociology.org/about/isa_code_of_ethics.htm
Membership in the ISA commits members to adhere to its code of ethics, but the ISA cautions that the fact that a particular conduct is not addressed specifically by the code does not mean the conduct is or is not ethical.

Appendix B

Sample Information Letter

[Name and address of university]
[Personal name, address, phone, date]

I wish to invite you to participate in my research that asks whether or not the research-ethics review process is changing the methodology and/ or topics of research undertaken by social scientists. This research will, for the first time, I hope, add to our understanding of how social-science research fares under research-ethics review. My project employs documentary analysis, interviews, focus groups, and published accounts of the experiences of researchers whose work were adjudicated by research ethics boards (REBs). The research involves interviewing both former and current members of REBs such as yourself, and conducting ethnographic research on REBs.

I have chosen ten universities across Canada where I intend to interview REB chairs. I hope to attend, with your approval, at least one session of an REB meeting at each university as a participant-observer to observe the consultative process of that meeting. I hope to discuss with you some of the more interesting cases that you believe might have a bearing on my research focus. I would welcome both your overall view on this matter, as well as your views on specific cases. With your approval I hope to use a tape recorder, which makes it easier to transcribe your views more accurately. I anticipate needing one to two hours for the session.

If you and members of the REB approve my attending a full session, I would be very interested in hearing about how social-science research proposals are considered by the members, from the manner of their deliberations. I hope to be as unobtrusive as possible and will take field notes (and not use a tape recorder). If by chance the REB session plans to discuss directly with me their views on social-science research proposals, I would welcome that, although I realize that pressures of time may preclude such a discussion.

I shall maintain strict confidentiality of all REB chairs and I will not reveal the personal name and institutional affiliation of the participants or of the specific REB. Similarly, if I have your (and the researcher's) permission to go over documents related to the ethics-review process, I shall not reveal the identity of the researcher in any given case—after all, I am interested in generic social processes, not in individuals per se. Naturally, any publications coming out of the research will not identify the participants, and all data will be aggregated and reported in such a way that individuals will not be recognized. The data will be safely stored in my office in a filing cabinet. Please let me know if you are interested in receiving an early draft of what I have written for publication, in which case I welcome receiving your further insights and ideas.

Both the transcriber and my student research assistant will be bound by these provisions. In selecting the focus groups of researchers, I will not choose the same universities where I am doing the REB element of the research, so as to avoid any perception that I might be checking out the activities of the ten REBs.

The Social Sciences and Humanities Research Council of Canada has provided me with a standard peer-reviewed research grant, from 2003 to 2006, for this project.

I thank you for your participation and look forward to establishing and then continuing our research relationship. I will respect your wish not to continue the research or interview if at any point you wish to withdraw from the research, in which case I will delete any data pertaining to the interview, without penalty. Please contact [name], Chair of my Department (at the same address), if you have any other queries about my research.

Appendix C

Further Reading

Blee, Kathleen M., and Ashley Currier. 2011. "Ethics Beyond the IRB: An Introductory Essay." *Qualitative Sociology* 34: 401–413.

Qualitative sociologists confront thorny ethical issues, many of which are beyond the scope of institutional review board procedures and protocols. This essay presents the broad themes of this special issue by reviewing major approaches to scholarly ethical practice, offering a set of orienting propositions, and introducing the contributions of and connections among the articles that follow.

Convery, Ian, and Diane Cox. 2012. "A Review of Research Ethics in Internet-based Research." *Practitioner Research in Higher Education* 6 (1): 50–57.

This article has a number of suggestions about doing research on Internet chat rooms, and describes the pros and cons of each one.

Eder, Donna, and William Corsaro. 1999. "Ethnographic Studies of Children and Youth: Theoretical and Ethical Issues." *Journal of Contemporary Ethnography* 28 (5): 520–531.

Given the fact that children and youth represent the future who will shape the society and culture, it is important to spell out the theoretical and ethical issues that involve research with them.

Fine, Gary Alan. 1993. "Ten Lies of Ethnography: Moral Dilemmas of Field Research." *Journal of Contemporary Ethnography* 22 (3): 267–294.

Illusions are essential for maintaining occupational reputation, but in the process they create a set of moral dilemmas. So it is with ethnographic work. This article describes the underside of ethnographic work: compromises that one frequently makes with idealized ethical standards. It argues that images of ethnographers—personal and public—are based on partial truths or self-deceptions. The focus is on three clusters of dilemmas: the classical virtues (the kindly ethnographer, the friendly ethnographer, and the honest ethnographer), technical skills (the precise ethnographer, the observant ethnographer, and the unobtrusive ethnographer), and the ethnographic self (the candid ethnographer, the chaste ethnographer, the fair ethnographer, and the literary ethnographer). Changes in ethnographic styles and traditions alter the balance of these deceptions but do not eliminate the need for methodological illusions.

Rivière, Dominique. 2011. "Looking from the Outside/In: Re-thinking Research Ethics Review." *Journal of Academic Ethics* 9: 193–204.

This paper explores the consent process from the author's point of view as both a qualitative researcher and a member of an ethics committee. She attempts to outline a new vision of research ethics.

Endnotes

1. To avoid the awkwardness of *hers and his* or *his/her*, we alternate gender terms between the chapters.

2. Howard S. Becker speaks extensively of this idea in his piece, "Whose Side Are We On?" (Becker, 1967).

3. Experienced writers employ all sorts of literary devices to convey layered interpretations of facts, including the tone of the written word or placing particular observations in an endnote.

4. Our textbook encourages the use of the "Information Letter" (see Appendix B) rather than consent forms signed by research participants. A number of ideas in this section about how some researchers handle situations where ethics and law might converge are derived from Mark Israel (2004).

5. As it turns out in this research, agencies did not have the staff to track down families of youth who were already living outside the home (Jansson and Benoit, 2006).

6. A random search through our bookcase for ethnographies generated thirty-three books. The average time for a research project to be converted into a book was 8.1 years. Of the thirty-three books, eight took at least twelve years. What we found is close to the research by Vicki Smith (2002: 228), who studied fifty research monographs and realized that it took 8.14 years on average after the start of fieldwork to see its appearance as a book.

7. Sensitive data would consist of information about racial or ethnic origin, political opinions, religious beliefs, memberships in organizations, health and illness, sex life, criminal record, etc. (Parry and Mauthner, 2004: 143).

8. Murray Wax (1980) offers one of the most insightful articles on fieldwork. He not only describes the process of fieldwork (during the Golden Age of this methodology) but provides valuable suggestions with regard to consent as event and process, studying what is already public, antagonistic fieldwork, hierachical entities, and gatekeepers.

9. Will van den Hoonaard was astonished to realize the he only used 7 percent of his interview transcripts in an early draft of his book about mapmakers (2013).

10. *Forum: Qualitative Social Research* has a special issue (2012, 13[1]) devoted to participatory action research.

11. Avril Maddrell has been researching the issue of women in geography. Her book *Complex Locations* (2009: 16–24) offers a string of helpful ethical insights when dealing with (auto)biographies, archives, oral histories, obituaries, and reviews. We warmly commend these passages.

12. See www.youtube.com/watch?v=TPAO-lZ4_hU&feature=related&mid=57 (accessed 16 January 2012).

13. See royal.pingdom.com/2012/01/17/internet-2011-in-numbers/ (accessed 23 June 2012).

14. We are deeply grateful to Riva Soucie, who provided us with valuable insights about the ethics of research related to photo elicitation, 12 January 2012. We have also relied on Wiles et al. (2012), who have provided a balanced discussion on this issue. Their article cites a number of key scholarly papers on this topic.

15. Those wishing to pursue the subject further should consult Lynn Blinn and Amanda Harrist (1991), Chalfen (1998), Clark-Ibañez (2004), Collier (1967), Dodman (2003), Evans (2000), Geoffroy (1990), Green and Kloos (2009), Harper (2002), Hurworth (2003), Markwell (2000), Rieger (1996), Sampson-Cordle (2001), and Wang (1996, 1997). I thank Riva Soucie for providing this helpful list.

16. See www.cbc.ca/asithappens/episode/2012/01/25/the-wednesday-edition-12 (accessed 3 February 2012).

17. See www.aaanet.org/stmts/irb.htm (accessed 31 June 2012).

18. When Will van den Hoonaard participated in the work of a committee charged with bringing the 1998 *TCPS* up to date and wrote chapter 10 of this policy document, the term *deception* in research was so widely used (and still is) that he had difficulty distinguishing among *deception, partial disclosure*, and *covert research. Deception* was the catchall phrase. However, as Chapter 8 in this book shows, there are indeed huge conceptual differences among these terms.

19. Roger Homan, in *The Ethics of Social Research* (1991: 96–126), devotes a long chapter to many eye-catching and interesting cases of covert research.

20. *TCPS 2* (2010) allows for this stage of the research without going through research-ethics review (Article 10.1).

21. The matter of taking away the researcher's choice was raised by Ted Palys, 31 July 2003.

22. Jeremy N. Block (2008) argues that there ought to be a disability representative on institutional review boards who is charged with representing the voice of persons with disabilities.

23. To avoid awkwardness, we simply write *organization(s)*, but we include institutions in our discussions.

24. Just think of trying to define "correctional institutions" not as prisons but as "cages for humans." The ideological basis would become suddenly quite transparent.

25. Nursing professor Kathleen M. Oberle wrote "Ethics in Qualitative Research" (2002) with medical practitioners in mind, showing them the basis, purpose, and methods of qualitative research.

26. Normally, the authors of cited works or references are also involved. It has been the contention of one of us that references should respect cited authors by using their full names, or the names that appear on their publications. This means that references in bibliographies should have the an author's first name written out in full (as is the case in this book) rather an abbreviation (unless the cited author also used abbreviations). The current APA (and other) referencing systems are guilty of this unethical practice—all for the sake of convenience.

27. One of the articles that garnered the highest number of coauthors was for a physics journal; there were 396 coauthors from 77 research institutions. The article was just over four pages in length (see https://oraweb.slac.stanford.edu/pls/slacquery/casepuppy.bbrdownload/paper.pdf?P_FRAME=DEST&P_DOC_ID=14820, Lake Louise Institute, 23 February 2011, accessed 5 April 2012). However, the article with the greatest number of authors appeared in another physics journal in 2008—with 2,926 authors from 169 research institutions (http://en.wikipedia.org/wiki/Academic_authorship, accessed 2 July 2012).

28. This section relies on http://en.wikipedia.org/wiki/Academic_authorship for some of its details.

29. Murray et al. (2012) discuss the ethics-review process when a PhD student wanted to share her "secrets of mothering" in her dissertation. Among some of the general studies on university ethics committees related to qualitative research, we find Clifford G. Christians (2000), Kevin D. Haggerty (2004), Julianne Cheek (2007), Gaile S. Cannella and Yvonna S. Lincoln (2007), and Judith Taylor and Matthew Patterson (2010).

30. There is an increasing number of articles, Facebook pages, and websites devoted to "slow scholarship." See, for example, www.facebook.com/groups/188202231458/ and www.slow-science.org/.

References

Aldred, Rachel. 2008. "Ethical and Political Issues in Contemporary Research Relationships." *Sociology* 42 (5): 887–903.

Anon. n.d. "Wigmore Criteria." Available at: www.sfu.ca/~palys/Wigmore. html. Accessed 3 Sept. 2012.

Anon. 2012. "Editorial: BC Decision Should Lead Others to Amend Oral-History Pacts." *Boston Globe*, 11 July 2012. Available at: www. bostonglobe.com/opinion/editorials/2012/07/11/universities-must-amend-oral-history-agreements/4RzAO3AGPoLRhwaFPjH5GM/story. html. Accessed 6 December 2012.

Association of Internet Researchers. 2002. *Ethical Decision-making and Internet Research.: Recommendations from the AoIR Ethics Working Committee.* Available at: www.aoir.org/reports/ethics.pdf. Accessed 28 December 2012.

Atkins-Idzi, Sandie. 1997. "Capitalists Cults: The Quasi-Religious Inter-actional Aspects of Multi-Level Marketing Organizations." Thesis proposal, 14 May. Department of Sociology. University of New Bruns-wick, Fredericton.

Atkinson, Paul. 1990. *The Ethnographic Imagination: Textual Constructions of Reality.* London: Routledge.

Baarts, Charlotte. 2009. "Stuck in the Middle: Research Ethics Caught Between Science and Politics." *Qualitative Research* 9 (4): 423–439.

Barton, Bernadette. 2011. "My Auto/Ethnographic Dilemma: Who Owns the Story." *Qualitative Sociology* 34 (3): 431–445.

Becker, Howard S. 1967. "Whose Side Are We On?" *Social Problems* 14: 239–248.

———. 1998. *Tricks of the Trade: How to Think About Your Research While You're Doing It.* Chicago: University of Chicago Press.

Becker, Howard S., Blanche Geer, Everett C. Hughes, and Anselm L. Strauss. 1961 [1973]. *Boys in White: Student Culture in Medical School.* Brunswick: Transactions.

Berg, Bruce L., and Howard Lune. 2012. *Qualitative Research Methods for the Social Sciences,* 8th edition. Boston: Allyn and Bacon.

Bhattacharya, Kakali. 2007. "Consenting to the Consent Form: What Are the Fixed and Fluid Understandings Between the Researcher and the Researched?" *Qualitative Inquiry* 13 (8): 1095–1115.

Blancett, Suzanne Smith. 1991. "The Ethics of Writing and Publishing." *Journal of Nursing Administration* 21 (5): 31–36.

Blee, Kathleen M., and Ashley Currier. 2011. "Ethics Beyond the IRB: An Introductory Essay." *Qualitative Sociology* 34: 401–413.

Blinn, Lynn, and Amanda W. Harrist. 1991."Combining Native Instant Photography and Photo-Elicitation." *Visual Anthropology* 4 (2): 175–192.

Block, Jeremy N. 2008. "Research on Disabled Populations: IRB Membership Considerations." Posted 23 February. Available at http://sciencepolicydev. blogspot.com/2008/02/research-on-disabled-populations-irb.html. Accessed 27 February 2008.

Blumer, Herbert G. 1969. *Symbolic Interactionism: Perspective and Method.* Englewood Cliffs, NJ: Prentice Hall.

Bosk, Charles L. 2001. "Irony, Ethnography, and Informed Consent." Pp. 199–220 in Barry Hoffmaster (ed.), *Bioethics in Social Context.* Philadelphia: Temple University Press.

Brajuha, Mario, and Lyle Hallowell. 1986. "Legal Intrusion and the Politics of Fieldwork: The Impact of the Brajuha Case. *Urban Life* 14 :454–478.

Bretag, Tracey, and Saadia Mahmud. 2009. "Self-Plagiarism or Appropriate Textual Re-Use?" *Journal of Academic Ethics* 7 (3): 193–205.

Bruckman, Amy. 2002. "Studying the Amateur Artist: A Perspective on Disguising Data Collected in Human Subjects Research on the Internet." *Ethics and Information Technology* 4: 217–231.

Caissie, Linda. 2006. *The Raging Grannies: Understanding the Role of Activism in the Lives of Older Women.* PhD Dissertation, University of Waterloo, Ontario.

Calvey, David. 2008. "The Art and Politics of Covert Research: Doing 'Situated Ethics' in the Field." *Sociology* 42: 905–918.

Cannella, Gaile S., and Yvonna S. Lincoln. 2007. "Predatory vs. Dialogic Ethics." *Qualitative Inquiry* 13 (3): 315–335.

Cassell, J. 1980. "Ethical Principles for Conducting Fieldwork." *American Anthropologist* 82: 28–41.

Chalfen, Richard. 1998. "Interpreting Family Photography as Pictorial Communication." Pp. 214–234 in Jon Prosser (ed.), *Image-based Research: A Sourcebook for Qualitative Researchers*. London: Falmer Press.

Cheek, Julianne. 2007. "Qualitative Inquiry, Ethics, and Politics of Evidence." *Qualitative Inquiry* 13 (8): 1051–1059.

Christians, Clifford G. 2000. "Ethics and Politics in Qualitative Research." Pp. 133–155 in Norman K. Denzin and Yvonna S. Lincoln (eds.), *Handbook of Qualitative Research*. Thousand Oaks, CA: Sage.

CIHR (Canadian Institutes of Health Research). 2012. "More About Knowledge Translation at CIHR." Updated 23 October. www.cihr-irsc. gc.ca/e/39033.html. Accessed 19 December 2012.

CIHR (Canadian Institutes of Health Research), Natural Sciences and Engineering Research Council, and the Social Sciences and Humanities Research Council. 2010. *Tri-Council Policy Statement on Ethical Conduct for Research Involving Humans,* 2nd ed. Ottawa, Ontario: Interagency Secretariat on Research Ethics.

Clark-Ibaez, Marisol. 2004. "Framing the Social World with Photo-Elicitation Interviews." *American Behavioural Scientist* 47 (12): 1507–1527.

Clarke, Dawne. 2010. *A Sociological Study of Scholarly Writing and Publishing: How Academics Produce and Share Their Research*. Lewiston, NY: The Edwin Mellen Press.

Cloke, Paul, Phil Cooke, Jenny Cursons, Paul Milbourne, and Rebekah Widdowfield. 2000. "Ethics, Reflexivity and Research: Encounters with Homeless People." *Ethics, Place, and Environment* 3 (2): 133–154.

Collier, John, Jr. 1967. *Visual Anthropology: Photography as a Research Method*. New York: Holt, Rinehart and Winston.

Collier, John, and Malcolm Collier. 1986. *Visual Anthropology: Photography as a Research Method*. Albuquerque: University of New Mexico Press.

Conn, Lesley Gotlib. 2008. "Ethics Policy as Audit in Canadian Clinical Settings: Exiling the Ethnographic Method." *Qualitative Research* 8 (4): 499–514.

Convery, Ian, and Diane Cox. 2012. "A Review of Research Ethics in Internet-based Research." *Practitioner Research in Higher Education* 6 (1): 50–57.

Corbin, Juliet, and Janice M. Morse, 2003. "The Unstructured Interactive Interview: Issues of Reciprocity and Risks when Dealing with Sensitive Topics." *Qualitative Inquiry* 9 (3): 335–354.

Cornwall, Andrea, and Rachel Jewkes. 1995. "What Is Participatory Research?" *Social Science and Medicine* 41 (12): 1667–1676.

Crow, Graham, Rose Wiles, Sue Heath, and Vikki Charles. 2006. "Research Ethics and Data Quality: The Implications of Informed Consent." *International Journal of Social Research Methodology* 9 (2): 83–95.

Davis, Fred. 1960. "Comment on 'Initial Interaction of Newcomers in Alcoholics Anonymous.'" *Social Problems* 8: 364–365.

Debro, Julius. 1986. "Dialogue with Howard S. Becker (1970): An Interview Conducted by Julius Debro." Pp. 25–46 in Howard S. Becker, *Doing Things Together: Selected Papers*. Evanston, IL: Northwestern University Press.

Denzin, Norman K., and Michael D. Giradina (eds.). 2007. *Ethical Futures in Qualitative Research: Decolonizing the Politics of Knowledge*. Walnut Creek, CA: Left Coast Press.

Denzin, Norman K., and Yvonna S. Lincoln (eds). 1994. *Handbook of Qualitative Research*. Thousand Oaks, CA: Sage.

Diamond, Timothy. 1992. *Making Gray Gold: Narratives of Nursing Home Care*. Chicago: University of Chicago Press.

Dodman, David R. 2003. "Shooting in the City: An Autophotographic Exploration of the Urban Environment in Kingston Jamaica." *Area* 35 (3): 293–304.

Doucet, Andrea. 2006. *Do Men Mother? Fathering, Care and Domestic Responsibility*. Toronto: University of Toronto Press.

Duneier, Mitchell. 2001. *Sidewalk*. New York: Farrar, Straus and Giroux.

du Toit, Brian M. 1980. "Ethics, Informed Consent, and Fieldwork." *Journal of Anthropological Research* 36 (3): 274–286.

Eder, Donna, and William Corsaro. 1999. "Ethnographic Studies of Children and Youth." *Journal of Contemporary Ethnography* 28 (5): 520–531.

Ellis, Carolyn. 2007. "Telling Secrets, Revealing Lives: Relational Ethics in Research with Intimate Others." *Qualitative Inquiry* 13 (1): 3–29.

Ellis, Carolyn, Christine E. Kiesinger, and Lisa M. Tillmann-Healy. 1997. "Interactive Interviewing: Talking about Emotional Experience." Pp. 119–149 in Rosanna Hertz (ed.), *Reflexivity and Voice*. Thousand Oaks, CA: Sage.

Ells, Carolyn. 2011. "Communicating Qualitative Research Study Designs to Research Ethics Review Boards." *The Qualitative Report* 16 (3): 881–891.

Emme, Michael J. 2008. "Photonovella and PhotoVoice." Pp. 622–624 in Lisa M. Given (ed.), *The Sage Encyclopedia of Qualitative Research Methods, Vol. 2*. Thousand Oaks, CA: Sage.

ESRC (Economic and Social Research Council). 2010. *Framework for Research Ethics*. London: UK Research Integrity Office Code of Practice for Research. Available at: www.esrc.ac.uk/_images/Framework_for_Research_Ethics_tcm8-4586.pdf. Accessed 19 July 2012.

Evans, Jessica. 2000. "Feminism and Photography: Languages of Exposure." Pp. 105–121 in Fiona Carson and Claire Pajackowsksa (eds.), *Feminism and Visual Culture*. Edinburgh: Edinburgh University Press.

Festinger, Leon, et al. 1956. *When Prophecy Fails*. New York: Harper and Row.

Fine, Gary Alan. 1993. "Ten Lies of Ethnography: Moral Dilemmas of Field Research." *Journal of Contemporary Ethnography* 22 (3): 267–294.

Frankel, Mark S., and Sanyin Siang. 1999. "Ethical and Legal Aspects of Human Subjects Research on the Internet: A Report of a Workshop, June 10–11, 1999." American Association for the Advancement of Science, November 1999. Available at: http://shr.aaas.org/projects/human_subjects/cyberspace/report.pdf. Accessed 28 December 2012.

Gans, Herbert J. 1967. *The Levittowners: Ways of Life and Politics in a New Suburban Community.* New York: Random House.

Geoffroy, Yannick. 1990. "Family Photographs: A Visual Heritage." *Visual Anthropology* 3 (4): 367–409.

Goffman, Erving. 2004 [1974]. "On Fieldwork." Transcribed and edited by L. H. Lofland. Pp. 147–153 in D. Weinberg (eds.), *Qualitative Research Methods.* Malden, MA: Blackwell.

Gouliquer, Lynne. 2000. "Negotiating Sexuality: Lesbians in the Canadian Military." Pp. 254–77 in Baukje Miedema, Janet M. Stoppard, and Vivian Anderson (eds.), *Women's Bodies, Women's Lives: Health, Well-being, and Body Image.* Toronto: Sumach Press.

Green, Eric, and Bret Kloos. 2009. "Facilitating Youth Participation in a Context of Forced Migration: A Photovoice Project in Northern Uganda." *Journal of Refugee Studies* 22.4: 460–482.

Griffin, Howard. 1977. *Black Like Me.* 2nd edition. Boston: Houghton Mifflin.

Guillemin, Marylis, and Lynn Gillam, 2004. "Ethics, Reflexivity, and 'Ethically Important Moments' in Research." *Qualitative Inquiry* 10: 261–280.

Haas, Jack, and Willilam Shaffir. 2009 [1987]. *Becoming Doctors: The Adoption of a Cloak of Competence.* Cowichan Bay, British Columbia: Jack Haas Publishing.

Habenstein, Robert W. 1954. "The Career of the Funeral Director." PhD Dissertation, University of Chicago.

Haggerty, Kevin D. 2004. "Ethics Creep: Governing Social Sciences Research in the Name of Ethics." *Qualitative Sociology* 27 (4): 391–414.

Halse, Christine, and Anne Honey. 2005. "Unraveling Ethics: Illuminating the Moral Dilemmas of Research Ethics." *Signs: Journal of Women in Culture and Society* 30 (4): 2141–2161.

Handelman, Don, and Elliott Leyton. 1978. *Bureaucracy and World View: Studies in the Logic of Official Interpretation.* Social and Economic Studies No. 22. St. John's, Newfoundland: ISER.

Harper, Douglas. 2002. "Talking About Pictures: A Case for Photo Elicitation." *Visual Studies* 17 (1): 13–26.

Harper, Melissa, and Patricia Cole. 2012. "Member Checking: Can Benefits Be Gained Similar to Group Therapy?" *The Qualitative Report* 17 (2): 510–517.

Harrison, Deborah (with seven collaborators). 2002. *The First Casualty: Violence Against Women in Canadian Military Communities.* Toronto: James Lorimer.

Harvey, William. 2009. *Methodological Approaches for Junior Researchers Interviewing Elites: A Multidisciplinary Perspective.* Working Paper Series No. 01.09. Vancouver, British Columbia: Economic Geography Research Group at the University of British Columbia. Available at: www.egrg.org. uk/pdfs/egrg_wp0109.pdf. Accessed 9 June 2012.

Helgeland, Ingeborg Marie. 2005. "'Catch 22' of Research Ethics: Ethical Dilemmas in Follow-Up Studies of Marginal Groups." *Qualitative Inquiry* 11 (4): 549–569.

Hochschild, Arlie R.1997. *The Time Bind: When Work Becomes Home and Home Becomes Work.* New York: Henry Holt.

Holland, Kate. 2007. "The Epistemological Bias of Ethics Review: Constraining Mental Health Research." *Qualitative Inquiry* 13: 895–913.

Holloway, Immy, and Stephanie Wheeler. 1995. "Ethical Issues in Qualitative Nursing Research." *Nursing Ethics* 2 (3): 223–232.

Homan, Roger. 1991. *The Ethics of Social Research.* London: Longman.

Humphreys, Laud 1970. *Tearoom Trade: Impersonal Sex in Public Places.* Chicago: Aldine.

Hurworth, Rosalind. 2003. "Photo-Interviewing for Research." *Social Research Update.* 40. Available at: http://sru.soc.surrey.ac.uk/SRU40.html. Accessed 28 December 2012.

Israel, Mark. 2004. *Ethics and the Governance of Criminological Research in Australia.* Sydney, Australia: NSW Bureau of Crime Statistics and Research.

Isserman, Maurice. 2012. "Op-Ed: The Poverty of an Idea." *New York Times,* 2 March.

Jansson, Mikael, and Cecilia Benoit, 2006. "Respect and Protect? Conducting Community-Academic Research with Street-Involved Youth." Pp. 175–189 in Bonnier Leadbeater, Elizabeth Banister, Cecilia Benoit, Mikael Jansson, Anne Marshall, and Ted Riecken (eds.), *Ethical Issues in Community-Based Research with Children and Youth.* Toronto: University of Toronto Press.

Jaschik, Scott. 2007. "Questions, Anger, and Dissent on Ethics Study." *Inside Higher Ed,* 30 November. Available at: www.insidehighered.com/ news/2007/11/30/anthro. Accessed 2 April 2012.

Jordan, Steve. 2008. "Participatory Action Research (PAR)." Pp. 601–604 in Lisa M. Given (ed.), *The Sage Encyclopedia of Qualitative Research Methods, Vol. 2.* Thousand Oaks, CA: Sage.

Kanter, Rosabeth Moss. 1977. *Men and Women of the Corporation.* New York: Basic Books.

Keegan, Sheila. 2008. "Photographs in Qualitative Research." Pp. 619–624 in Lisa M. Given (ed.), *The Sage Encyclopedia of Qualitative Research Methods, Vol. 2.* Thousand Oaks, CA: Sage.

Kemmis, Stephen, and Robin McTaggart. 2000. "Participatory Action Research: Communicative Action in the Public Sphere." Pp. 559–603 in

N. Denzin and Y. Lincoln (eds.), *Handbook of Qualitative Research*. Thousand Oaks, CA: Sage.

Kennedy, Joyce Ellen. 2005. "Grey Matter: Ambiguities and Complexities of Ethics in Research." *Journal of Academic Ethics* 3 (2–4): 143–158.

Khanlou, Nazilla, and Elizabeth Peter. 2005. "Participatory Action Research: Considerations for Ethical Review." *Social Science and Medicine* 60: 2333–2340.

Khyatt, M. D. 1992. *Lesbian Teachers: An Invisible Presence*. New York: State University of New York Press.

Kitchin, Heather A. 2003. "The Tri-Council Policy Statement and Research in Cyberspace: Research Ethics, the Internet, and Revising a 'Living Document.'" *Journal of Academic Ethics* 1: 397–418.

Kitchin, Heather A. 2007. *Research Ethics and the Internet: Negotiating Canada's Tri-Council Policy Statement*. Halifax, Nova Scotia: Fernwood.

Kraut, Robert, Judith Olson, Mahzarin Banaji, Amy Bruckman, Jeffrey Cohen, and Mick Couper. 2004. "Psychological Research Online: Report of Board of Scientific Affairs' Advisory Group on the Conduct of Research on the Internet." *American Psychologist* 59 (2): 105–117.

Lakes, Kimberley D., Elaine Vaughan, Marissa Jones, Wylie Burke, Dean Baker, and James M. Swanson. 2012. "Diverse Perceptions of the Informed Consent Process: Implications for the Recruitment and Participation of Diverse Communities in the National Children's Study." *American Journal of Community Psychology* 49: 215–232.

Leadbeater, Bonnie, and Kathleen Glass. 2006. "Including Vulnerable Populations in Community-Based Research: New Directions for Ethics Guidelines and Ethics Research." Pp. 248–266 in Bonnie Leadbeater, Elizabeth Banister, Cecilia Benoit, Mikael Jansson, Anne Marshall, and Ted Riecken (eds.), *Ethical Issues in Community-Based Research with Children and Youth*. Toronto: University of Toronto Press.

Lewis, Oscar. 1961. *The Children of Sanchez: Autobiography of a Mexican Family*. New York: Vintage.

Liebow, Elliot. 1993. *Tell Them Whom I Am: The Lives of Homeless Women*. Toronto: Macmillan.

Lofland, John F. 1966. *Doomsday Cult: A Study of Conversion, Proselytization and Maintenance of Faith*. Englewood Cliffs, NJ: Prentice Hall.

Macdonald, Mary Ellen, and Franco A. Carnevale. 2008. "Qualitative Health Research and the IRB: Answering the 'So What?' with Qualitative Inquiry." *Journal of Academic Ethics* 6: 1–5.

Maddrell, Avril. 2009. *Complex Locations: Women's Geographical Work in the UK, 1850–1970*. Oxford: Wiley-Blackwell.

Malone, Ruth E., Valeria B. Yerger, Carol McGruder, and Erika Froelicher. 2006. "'It's Like Tuskegee in Reverse': A Case Study of Ethical Tensions in

Institutional Review Board Review of Community-Based Participatory Research." *Health Policy and Ethics* 96 (11): 1914–1919.

Markwell, K. 2000. "Photo Documentation and Analysis as Research Strategies in Human Geography." *Australian Geographical Studies* 38 (1): 91–98.

Marzano, Marco. 2007. "Informed Consent, Deception, and Research Freedom in Qualitative Research." *Qualitative Inquiry* 13: 417–436.

Mayan, Maria J. 2009. *Essentials of Qualitative Research Inquiry*. Walnut Creek, CA: Left Coast Press.

McCloskey, Rose. 2011. "The 'Mindless' Relationship between Nursing Homes and Emergency Departments: What Do Bourdieu and Freire Have to Offer?" *Nursing Inquiry* 18 (2): 154–164.

McIntosh, Michele J., and Janice M. Morse. 2009. "Institutional Review Boards and the Ethics of Emotion." Pp. 81–107 in Norman K. Denzin and Michael D. Giradina (eds.), *Qualitative Inquiry and Social Justice: Towards a Politics of Hope*. Walnut Creek, CA: Left Coast Press.

McIntyre, Lisa J. 2002. *The Practical Skeptic: Readings in Sociology*. Boston: McGraw Hill.

Miller, Tina, and Linda Bell. 2002. "Consenting to What?: Ethical Issues of Access, Gate-keeping, and 'Informed' Consent." Pp. 53–69 in Melanie Mauthner, Maxine Birch, Julie Jessop, and Tina Miller (eds.), *Ethics in Qualitative Research*. London: Sage.

Mills, C. Wright. 1976 [1959]. *The Sociological Imagination*. New York: Oxford University Press.

Mintz, Steven, Arline Savage, and Richard Carter. 2010. "Commercialism and Universities: An Ethical Analysis." *Journal of Academic Ethics* 8 (1): 1–19.

Morgan, David L. 1988. *Focus Groups as Qualitative Research*. Newbury Park, CA: Sage.

Morse, Janice M. 1998. "The Contracted Relationship: Ensuring Protection of Anonymity and Confidentiality." *Qualitative Health Research* 8 (3): 301–303.

———. 2001. "Interviewing the Ill." Pp. 317–328 in Jaber F. Gubrium and James A. Holstein (eds.), *Handbook of Interview Research*. Thousand Oaks, CA: Sage.

———. 2002. "Editorial: Writing My Own Experience." *Qualitative Health Research* 12 (9): 1159–1160.

———. 2008. "Does Informed Consent Interfere with Induction?" *Qualitative Health Research* 18 (4): 439–440.

Morse, Janice M., M. Barrett, M. Mayan, K. Olson, and J. Spiers. 2002. "Verification Strategies for Establishing Reliability and Validity in Qualitative Research." *International Journal of Qualitative Methods* 1(2): 1–19.

Morse, Janice M., Linda Niehaus, Stanley Varnhagen, Wendy Austin, and Michele McIntosh. 2008. "Qualitative Researchers' Conceptualizations of the Risks Inherent in Qualitative Interviews." Pp. 195–217 in Norman K.

Denzin and Michael D. Giardina (eds.), *Qualitative Inquiry and the Politics of Evidence*. Walnut Creek, CA: Left Coast Press.

MRC (Medical Research Council), Natural Sciences and Engineering Research Council, and the Social Sciences and Humanities Research Council. 1998. *Tri-Council Policy Statement on Ethical Conduct for Research Involving Humans*. Ottawa, Ontario: Public Works and Government Services Canada.

Murray, Elizabeth, and Robert Dingwall. 2002. "The Ethics of Ethnography." Pp. 339–351 in Paul Atkinson, Amanda Coffey, Sara Delamont, John Lofland, and Lyn Lofland (eds.), *Handbook of Ethnography*. London: Sage.

Murray, Lee, Debbie Pushor, and Pat Renihan. 2012. "Reflections on the Ethics-Approval Process." *Qualitative Inquiry* 18(1): 43–54.

Murray, Stephen O. 2005. "American Anthropologists Discover Peasants." *Histories of Anthropology Annual, Vol. 1*. Lincoln: University of Nebraska Press.

National Commission for the Protection of Human Subjects of Biomedical and Behavioral Research. 1979. *The Belmont Report: Ethical Principles and Guidelines for the Protection of Human Subjects of Research*. Washington, DC: Department of Health, Education, and Welfare.

NHMRC (National Health and Medical Research Council). 2007. *National Statement on Ethical Conduct in Human Research*. Canberra: Government of Australia. Available at: www.nhmrc.gov.au/_files_nhmrc/publications/attachments/e72.pdf. Accessed 31 June 2012.

Nind, Melanie. 2011. "Participatory Data Analysis: A Step Too Far?" *Qualitative Research* 11 (4): 349–363.

NSF (National Science Foundation). 2002. Frequently Asked Questions and Vignettes: Interpreting the Common Rule for the Protection of Human Subjects for Behavioral and Social Science Research. Washington, DC: NSF Policy Office. Available at: http://www.nsf.gov/bfa/dias/policy/hsfaqs.jsp. Accessed 19 December 2012.

Oakley, Ann. 1981. "Interviewing Women: A Contradiction in Terms." Pp. 30–61 in Helen Roberts (ed.), *Doing Feminist Research*. London: Routledge.

Oberle, Kathleen. 2002. "Ethics in Qualitative Research." *Annals RCPSC* 35 (8): 563–566.

Odendahl, Teresa, and Aileen M. Shaw. 2001. "Interviewing Elites." Pp. 299–316 in Jaber F. Gubrium and James A. Holstein (eds.), *Handbook of Interview Research*. Thousand Oaks, CA: Sage.

Ogden, Russel. 2008. "Confidentiality." Pp. 110–111 in Lisa M. Given (ed.), *The Sage Encyclopedia of Qualitative Research Methods, Vol. 1*. Los Angeles: Sage.

Orton-Johnson, Kate. 2010. "Ethics in Online Research: Evaluating the ESR Framework for Research Ethics Categorization of Risk." *Sociological Research Online* 14 (4): 13 ff.

Palys, Ted, and John Lowman. 2001. "Commentary: Social Research With Eyes Wide Shut: The Limited Confidentiality Dilemma." *Canadian Journal of Criminology* 43: 255–267.

Parker, Michael. 2007. "Ethnography/Ethics." *Social Science and Medicine* 65: 2248–2259.

Parry, Marc. 2011. "Harvard Researchers Accused of Breaching Students' Privacy." *Chronicle of Higher Education* 57(41): A1–A8, A9.

Parry, Odette, and Natasha S. Mauthner. 2004. "Whose Data Are They Anyway?: Practical, Legal, and Ethical Issues in Archiving Qualitative Research Data." *Sociology* 38 (1): 139–152.

Piquemal, Nathalie. 2001. "Free and Informed Consent in Research Involving Native American Communities." *American Indian Culture and Research Journal* 25 (1): 65–79.

Poulin, Carmen. 2001. "The Military Is the Wife and I Am the Mistress: Partners of Lesbians in the Canadian Military." *Atlantis* 26 (1): 65–76.

Powdermaker, Hortense. 1967. *Stranger and Friend: The Way of an Anthropologist.* New York: W.W. Norton.

Pratt, Michael G. 2000. "The Good, the Bad, and the Ambivalent: Managing Identification among Amway Distributors." *Administrative Science Quarterly* 45 (3): 456–493.

PRE (Panel on Research Ethics). 2011. "Consent." Available at: www.pre.ethics.gc.ca/eng/policy-politique/interpretations/consent-consentement/. Accessed 28 September 2012.

Redfield, Robert. 1971. *The Little Community/Peasant Society and Culture.* Chicago: University of Chicago Press.

Reinharz, Shulamit. 1993. *On Becoming a Social Scientist.* 4th edition. New Brunswick, NJ: Transaction.

Rieger, Jon H. 1996. "Photographing Social Change." *Visual Sociology* 11 (1): 5–49.

Rivière, Dominique. 2011. "Looking from the Outside/In: Re-thinking Research Ethics Review." *Journal of Academic Ethics* 9: 193–204.

Roach, Jack L., and Orville R. Gursslin. 1967. "An Evaluation of the Concept 'Culture of Poverty.'" *Social Forces* 45 (3): 383–392..

Rubenstein, Paul. 2012. "Why (and How) the Growth of Social Media Has Created Opportunities for Qualitative Research in Organizational Development." Society for Industrial and Organizational Psychology. Available at: http://ht.ly/8KQ4O. Accessed 5 February 2012.

Russell, Cherry. 1999. "Interviewing Vulnerable Old People: Ethical and methodological Implications of Imagining Our Subjects." *Journal of Aging Studies* 13 (4): 403–418.

Sampson-Cordle, Alice Vera. 2001. "Exploring the Relationship Between a Small Rural School in Northeast Georgia and Its Community: An Image-Based Study Using Participant-Produced Photographs." PhD Dissertation. University of Georgia, Athens, GA.

Schrag, Zachary. 2010. *Ethical Imperialism: Institutional Review Boards and the Social Sciences, 1965–2009.* Baltimore, MD: The Johns Hopkins University Press.

Scheper-Hughes, Nancy. 2002. "Commodity Fetishism in Organs Trafficking." Pp. 31–62 in Nancy Scheper-Hughes and Loïc Wacquant (eds.), *Commodifying Bodies.* London: Sage.

Scott, Craig R. 2005. "Anonymity in Applied Communication Research: Tensions Between IRBs, Researchers, and Human Subjects." *Journal of Applied Communication Research* 33 (3): 242–257.

Secretary of U.S. Department of Health and Human Services. 2009. "Minutes of the Secretary's Advisory Committee on Human Research Protections." 27–28 October, Arlington, VA. Available at: www.hhs.gov/ohrp/sachrp/mtgings/mtg10–09/minutes_.html. Accessed 19 July 2012.

Seifert, Tim, and M. Shute. 2005. "On Promising Anonymity and Confidentiality in Research." St. John's, Newfoundland: Memorial University of Newfoundland.

Shopes, Linda. 2002. "Oral History Interviewing, Institutional Review Boards, and Human Subjects." Paper presented to the Organization of American Historians Meeting, Washington, DC. April.

Sieber, Joan E., Rebecca Iannuzzo, and Beverly Rodriguez. 1995. "Deception Methods in Psychology: Have They Changed in 23 Years?" *Ethics and Behavior* 5 (1): 67–85.

Silverman, David. 1993. *Interpreting Qualitative Data: Methods for Analyzing Talk, Text, and Interaction.* London: Sage.

Smith, Vicki. 2002. "Ethnographies of Work and the Work of Ethnographers." Pp. 220–233 in Paul Atkinson, Amanda Coffey, Sarqa Delamont, John Lofland, and Lyn Lofland (eds.), *Handbook of Ethnography.* London: Sage.

Smythe, William E., and Maureen J. Murray. 2000. "Owning the Story: Ethical Considerations in Narrative Research." *Ethics and Behavior* 10 (4): 311–336.

Soucie, Riva. 2012. Personal communication with author.

Spicker, Paul. 2011. "Ethical Covert Research." *Sociology* 45 (1): 118–133.

SSHWC (Social Sciences and Humanities Research Ethics Special Working Group). 2004. *Giving Voice to the Spectrum.* Report prepared by the Social Sciences and Humanities Special Working Committee to the Interagency Advisory Panel on Research Ethics. Ottawa, Ontario. June.

———. 2007. *Continuing the Dialogue on Privacy and Confidentiality.* Report prepared by the Social Sciences and Humanities Special Working Committee to the Interagency Advisory Panel on Research Ethics. Ottawa, Ontario. June.

Stanford Encyclopedia of Philosophy, The. 2012. "Internet Research Ethics." Published 22 June. Available at: http://plato.stanford.edu/entries/ethics-internet-research/#HumSubRes. Accessed 17 July 2012.

Stark, Laura. 2011. *Behind Closed Doors: IRBs and the Making of Ethical Research.* Chicago: University of Chicago Press.

Swauger, Melissa. 2011. "Afterword: The Ethics of Risk, Power, and Representation." *Qualitative Sociology* 34: 497–502.

Taylor, Judith, and Matthew Patterson. 2010. "Autonomy and Compliance: How Qualitative Sociologists Respond to Institutional Ethical Oversight." *Qualitative Sociology* 33: 161–183.

Thompson, S. Anthony. 2002. "My Researcher-friend? My Friend the Researcher? My Friend, My Researcher?: Conceptual and Procedural Issues of Informed Consent in Qualitative Research Methods for Persons with Developmental Disabilities." Pp. 95–106 in Will C. van den Hoonaard (ed.), *Walking the Tightrope: Ethical Issues for Qualitative Researchers.* Toronto: University of Toronto Press.

Thorne, Barrie. 1980. "'You Still Takin' Notes?': Fieldwork and Problems on Informed Consent." *Social Problems* 27 (3): 284–297.

Tillmann-Healy, Lisa M. 2003. "Friendship as Method." *Qualitative Inquiry* 9 (5): 729–749.

Tolich, Martin. 2004. "Internal Confidentiality: When Confidentiality Assurances Fail Relational Informants." *Qualitative Sociology* 27 (1): 101–106.

Tolich, Martin, and Maureen H. Fitzgerald. 2006. "If Ethics Committees Were Designed for Ethnography." *Journal of Empirical Research on Human Research Ethics* 1 (2): 71–78.

United Nations. 1948. *The Universal Declaration of Human Rights.* New York: General Assembly, United Nations.

United States Department of Health and Human Services. 2009. "Code of Federal Regulations: Title 45, Public Welfare, Part 46, Protection of Human Subjects." Available at: www.hhs.gov/ohrp/humansubjects/guidance/45cfr46.html. Accessed 18 July 2012.

———. 2011. "Meeting of the Secretary's Advisory Committee on Human Research Protections (SACHRP). Tuesday, March 8, 2011–Wednesday, March 9, 2011." Washington, DC. Available at: www.hhs.gov/ohrp/sachrp/mtgings/mtg03–11/march2011minutes.pdf. Accessed 31 June 2012.

Vaillancourt, Tracy, and Violetta Igneski. 2006. "The Study of Suicidality among Children and Youth: Preliminary Recommendations and Best Practices." Pp. 207–218 in Bonnie Leadbeater, Elizabeth Banister, Cecilia

Benoit, Mikael Jansson, Anne Marshall, and Ted Riecken (eds.), *Ethical Issues in Community-Based Research with Children and Youth*. Toronto: University of Toronto Press.

van den Hoonaard, Deborah K. 2001. *The Widowed Self: The Older Woman's Journey through Widowhood*. Waterloo, Ontario: Wilfrid Laurier University Press.

———. 2009. "Moving Toward a Three-Way Intersection in Translational Research: A Sociological Perspective." *Qualitative Health Research* 19: 1783–1787.

———. 2010. *By Himself: The Older Man's Experience of Widowhood*. Toronto: University of Toronto Press.

van den Hoonaard, Deborah, and Will van den Hoonaard. 2006. *The Equality of Women and Men: The Experience of the Bahá'í Community of Canada*. Douglas, New Brunswick: Deborah and Will van den Hoonaard.

van den Hoonaard, Will C. 1972. "Local-level Autonomy: A Case Study of an Icelandic Fishing Community." M.A. Thesis. Department of Sociology, Memorial University of Newfoundland. St. John's, Newfoundland. June. 175 pp.

———. 1991. *Silent Ethnicity: The Dutch of New Brunswick*. Fredericton, New Brunswick: New Ireland Press.

———. 1996. *The Origins of the Bahá'í Community of Canada, 1898–1948*. Waterloo, Ontario: Wilfrid Laurier University Press.

———. 2001. "Is Research-Ethics Review a Moral Panic?" *Canadian Review of Sociology and Anthropology* 38 (1): 19–36.

———. 2002. *Walking the Tightrope: Ethical Issues for Qualitative Researchers*. Toronto: University of Toronto Press.

———. 2003. "Is Anonymity an Artifact in Ethnographic Research?" *Journal of Academic Ethics* 1 (2): 141–151.

——— (guest editor). 2006. *The Ethics Trapeze: Journal of Academic Ethics* 4.

———. 2011. *The Seduction of Ethics: Transforming the Social Sciences*. Toronto: University of Toronto Press.

———. 2013. *Map Worlds: A History of Women in Cartography*. Waterloo, Ontario: Wilfrid Laurier University Press (forthcoming).

Van Maanen, John. 1983. "The Moral Fix: On the Ethics of Fieldwork." Pp. 269–287 in Robert M. Emerson (ed.), *Contemporary Field Research*. Prospect Heights, IL: Waveland Press.

———. 1988. *Tales of the Field: On Writing Ethnography*. Chicago: University of Chicago Press.

Vidich, Arthur J., J. Bensman, and Maurice R. Stein (eds). 1964. *Reflections on Community Studies*. New York: Harper and Row.

Wang, Caroline. 1997. "Photovoice: Concept, Methodology, and Use for Participatory Needs Assessment." *Health Education and Behaviour* 24 (3): 369–387.

Wang, Caroline, Mary Ann Burris, and Xiang Yue Ping. 1996. "Chinese Village Women as Visual Anthropologists: A Participatory Approach to Reaching Policymakers." *Social Science and Medicine* 42 (10): 1391–1400.

Wax, Murray L. 1980. "Paradoxes of 'Consent' to the Practice of Fieldwork." *Social Problems* 27 (3): 272–283.

Wichmann, Cherami, and Kelly Taylor. 2004. *Federally Sentenced Women in Administrative Segregation: A Descriptive Analysis.* Ottawa, Ontario: Research Branch Correctional Service Canada. 26pp.

Whyte, William F. 1955 [1943]. *Street Corner Society.* Chicago: University of Chicago Press.

Wilde, Verina. 1992. "Controversial Hypothesis on the Relationship Between Researcher and Informant in Qualitative Research." *Journal of Advanced Nursing* 17: 234–242.

Wiles, Rose, Vikki Charles, Graham Crow, and Sue Heath. 2006. "Researching Researchers: Lessons for Research Ethics." *Qualitative Research* 6 (3): 283–299.

Wiles, Rose, Amanda Coffey, Judy Robinson, and Sue Heath. 2012a. "Anonymisation and Visual Images: Issues of Respect, 'Voice,' and Protection." *International Journal of Social Research Methodology* 15 (1): 41–53.

Wiles, Rose, Amanda Coffey, Judy Robinson, and Jon Prosser. 2012b. "Ethical Regulation and Visual Methods: Making Visual Research Impossible or Developing Good Practice?" *Sociological Research Online* 17 (1). Available at: www.socresonline.org.uk/17/1/8.html. Accessed 4 April 2012.

Williamson, Graham R., and Sue Prosser. 2002. "Action Research: Politics, Ethics, and Participation." *Journal of Advanced Nursing* 40 (5): 587–593.

Wolf, Daniel R. 1991. *The Rebels: A Brotherhood of Outlaw Bikers.* Toronto: University of Toronto Press.

Yuile, Amy, Debra Pepler, Wendy Craig, and Jennifer Connolly. 2006. "The Ethics of Peeking Behind the Fence: Issues Related to Studying Children's Aggression and Victimization." Pp. 70–89 in Bonnie Leadbeater, Elizabeth Banister, Cecilia Benoit, Mikael Jansson, Anne Marshall, and Ted Riecken (eds.), *Ethical Issues in Community-Based Research with Children and Youth.* Toronto: University of Toronto Press.

Zerubavel, Eviatar. 1979. *Patterns of Time in Hospital Life: A Sociological Perspective.* Chicago: University of Chicago Press.

Zinger, Ivan, and Cherami G. Wichmann. 1999. *The Psychological Effects of 60 Days in Administrative Segregation.* Research Report R-#85. Ottawa, Ontario: Correctional Service of Canada.

Index